A Chronicle of Easington Colliery

Mary N. Bell

Copyright © 2014 Mary N. Bell

All rights reserved.

ISBN: 1501025481
ISBN-13: 978-1501025488

DEDICATION

To my three children Christine, Margaret and Jimmy, and my late husband Jim and dearly loved grandson Stuart.

ACKNOWLEDGMENTS

Thanks to my family and friends who encouraged me. Also to friends in the Easington Writers particularly to Terry Dobson who designed the cover and helped me get this book into print.

Thank you to Durham Miners Union, Redhills, Durham City for allowing me to go through lots and lots of old minutes with many visits to compile my list of men killed at Easington pit.

Thanks also to Harry Barnes MP for North East Derbyshire, 1987 – 2005 also to Dr. David Boyes, County Councillor for Easington Division for providing forewords. Thank you Harry for your encouragement and the various e mails you sent me and the info when you found other men killed at Easington pit bringing my list from 182 to 192.

Special thanks to my late husband Jim who spent many hours telling me of his life in Easington Colliery and his time in the Royal Navy in the 2nd World War.

If I have forgotten anyone, Thank you.

Mary N. Bell

FOREWORD

By Harry Barnes

This book is a remarkable achievement.

Too often we have to make do and mend when examining the nature of life in a working class community. In autobiographies, established writers or celebrities who come from such backgrounds may hand some snippets from their formative years. Then historians may report on research material which they have unearthed. But unfortunately, these are all just bits and pieces. For as Peter Crookson pointed out in his book *The Pitmen's Requiem* (Northumbria Press 2010), working class people themselves seldom keep a "shoebox in the wardrobe" in which they have stored key source material about their family and community activities. So much of what we need to know about such communities gets missed or remains shrouded in generalisations.

Thankfully Mary Bell is a solid exception to the rule which Peter Crookston pointed to. Although she has collected together far more material about her community than that which a mere shoebox could accommodate. Mary was born in Easington Colliery in County Durham in 1930. It was only after the pit closed in 1993 and the bulldozers were later coming to knock down former Colliery houses in the area in which they lived, that she and her late husband Jim moved to a bungalow just two miles away at nearby Horden Colliery. But she never really left Easington, for she could not keep away from it. One of the solid links she developed was with the group of "Easington Writers"; where she came to contribute poems and articles for their fine publication *Shrugging Off the Wind* (2010).

Furthermore, Mary has an exceptional memory. Yet she does not just draw from her own experiences, for throughout her life she has sought (and retained) information from friends and relatives. On top of which she has conducted original research into Easington Colliery's past via avenues such as Durham Miners' Association and Beamish Museum. Her efforts are fully revealed in this book. First in her fine chronology of Easington Colliery's history, then finally when she traces the details about the 193 men and boys who were killed during the lifetime of the local pit. She has kept, compiled and used a stack of key information, which would fill masses of those shoe-boxes.

Mary has, however, done far more than keep records which others can turn to. In this book, she has used her store of information to illustrate and explain the nature of the area's solid working class community, whose life before the closure of the pit in 1993 rested overwhelmingly upon the mine's existence. For only a year after production had first got underway at the pit, her husband's grandparents and their three sons had moved into a Colliery house just across the road to the pit itself. Then by she was born, her parents and elder sister were already settled into local Colliery life.

The Colliery area that she was born into was then at its peak population of ten thousand. This population fell somewhat afterwards, thanks to the spread of birth control techniques. But it was the closure of the pit in 1993 which had the biggest impact on its make up. Its current population now being under half of the peak shown via the 1931 Census.

Mary tells how key events shaped the life of her community. It was often a school of hard knocks. There was the impact of the First World War (see the local War Memorials for the many former miners killed in action) and the serious influenza epidemic at its close. This was followed by a series of industrial disputes culminating in the lengthy Miners' Strike of 1926; then came short time working as a consequence of the 1931 economic crisis. From Mary's direct experiences as a young girl, we find out what local life was like during the Second World War. Then just as everything settled down to a form of relative post-war prosperity, Easington was hit by a devastating pit disaster in 1951 which killed 83 men. Later significant industrial unrest returned, culminating in the major strike of 1984-85 and then the closing of the pit in 1993- plus its consequences.

But these are merely the broad facts, Mary explains the key elements – what these facts mean in terms of the nature and quality of life in her community. She can do this because she is a full insider. I am like many others, in what is now often too much of a mobile society. It is a world in which people often feel obliged to uproot themselves and where they may eventually find fresh communal connections. I left Easington

Colliery over 50 years ago and finally settled in North Derbyshire. I have dabbled in writing three short articles about my old roots covering from 1899 to 1935, which are the years before my birth – often with the help of Mary's records. But Mary has now herself covered the broad sweep in both key detail and via the understanding that can only come from experience and involvement.

If many communities are short of "shoeboxes in their wardrobes", then let us hope there are those who read this book who will decide to follow Mary's alternative example. The more we know what daily life is like (and has been) in differing neighbourhoods, the better we understand the strengths we need to nurture and the factors we need to tackle.

Harry Barnes
Formally, MP for North East Derbyshire, 1987 – 2005.

FOREWORD

By Dr. David Boyes

It has been said that if Blackpool Tower could somehow represent the entire time that the world has been in existence, then the time man has been on the planet is equivalent to about three inches at the top of the flagpole that sits at the top of the tower. By that sort of reckoning the hundred years or so that the mining communities of East Durham have been in existence could be represented by a speck of dust on top of the flag.

During those hundred years though, however brief temporally it has been in a relative sense, a unique East Durham mentality has been forged. Customs and ways of life peculiar to mining communities in the eastern part of County Durham have entered into common parlance.

But how do we interpret what has happened in East Durham over the last hundred years? Undoubtedly in years to come it will be the chroniclers and historians who will try to make sense of the tumultuous times that coal has produced in the area. However, we must not forget the poets and novelists, such as Mary Bell, who attempt to explore the human relationships at the heart of the mining communities, for their contributions will go a long way to unearthing the essence of life in East Durham when coal was more than just a commodity to be dug up.

Dr. David Boyes
County Councillor
Easington Division.

COAL DUST IN MY VEINS.

by Mary N. Bell

Pits, miners, coal,
Companions of my life,
Proud pitman's daughter,
Loyal colliers wife,
Gallower, kist, pit prop,
Hewer, stoneman, putter,
Were the very first words,
I was heard to utter,
Deputy grandad,
Easington born and bred,
Poems and stories of coal,
stockpiled in my head,
In hundreds of years time,
when they dig up my remains,
Descendants will find I have
COAL DUST IN MY VEINS.

THREE CENTURIES OF EASINGTON COLLIERY.

LIFE IN EASINGTON COLLIERY IN THE TWENTIETH CENTURY.

I began to write this book in 1999 and finished it in 2012.

The history of Easington Colliery has always interested me from my father telling me 30 years before I was born Easington Colliery was green fields. From fields we became a community all due to the sinking of the pit in 1900. I was born into a booming and growing Easington Colliery. My father told me tales of the frozen man and that the North Sea had once been called the German Ocean. I thought these were Fairy stories but later found them to be true. . This is my story of my life in the twentieth century and the history from 1836 – 2012

Easington in 1836 was land that sloped down to the sea from Easington Village. There were quarries and a few farms in the area and fields. I imagine excitement was in the air when engineers arrived to start to sink a shaft to open a coal mine. The site was about a quarter of a mile from the coast in Seaside Lane, so called because it was the lane from Easington Village to the sea. However a band of sand was discovered and the work was abandoned.

Easington Coal Company in 1899 decided to try again this time nearer the sea almost on the cliff tops.

IMPORTANT DATES OF EASINGTON COLLIERY.

1899 **April 11** First sod cut by Miss Barwick of Thimberly Hall. Shaft sinking commenced and was much delayed by water encountered in the 500ft. of limestone which overlies the coal seams. The sinking was suspended for a while due to financial difficulties. When sinking the shaft FRENCH engineers could not cope with the water, sand and limestone they encountered. BELGIAN engineers were brought in but failed to make any progress. A freezing method was used.

1904 **28th November.** While a shift of sinkers were in the shaft, water broke in. The men climbed into a hopper (a large metal bucket) in which they had descended. One man volunteered to stay behind to give signals to the surface. His name Robert Atkinson and he lost his life. His body remained in the shaft for 4 years and 3 months. He was buried in Easington Village cemetery February 20th 1909 as there was no cemetery in Easington colliery. One opened in 1923.

The north pit was finished freezing by GERMAN contractors in 1909. Miners came from all parts to the new pit opened by Easington Coal Company, Weardale Offices, Spennymoor.

1903   **19th March.** Easington District Council offices opened at Easington Village.
Demolished for safety.

1904   **28th November.** While a shift of sinkers were in the shaft, water broke in. The men climbed into a hopper (a large metal bucket) in which they had descended. One man volunteered to stay behind to give signals to the surface. His name Robert Atkinson and he lost his life. (Reported in Durham Advertiser 02.12.1904) his body remained in the shaft for 4years and 3 months. (Reported in Durham Chronicle 26.02.1909) buried in Easington Village cemetery February 20th 1909 as there was no cemetery in Easington colliery. The colliery cemetery opened in 1923.

1905   **1st April.** Railway line Hartlepool to Seaham opened running through Easington Colliery.

1907   Work on shaft resumed by German engineers.

1909   Body of R. Atkinson recovered frozen in ice.

1909   **September 17th.** North pit finished freezing. Building of Colliery houses started Southside.

1910 **February 1st.** Pit buzzer blown for the first time.
July 8th Reached first working seam
September 14th. Small cages put into North pit shaft.
September 15th. First coals drawn.
September 19th First coals for sale left the colliery.
Haswell co-operative store opened on site where Sherburn Hill store replaced it. Next to Infant and Junior Schools

1911 **April 3rd.** Colliery time clock started.
November 25th. Cages put into South pit shaft.

1912 **January 15th.** First Easington coal shipped from Seaham.
Jan 29th South pit started to draw coal.
July 1st. Railway station opened for passenger service.
July 20th. Working men's club opened for membership.
July 21st Miners' Hall opened.
Empire cinema opened.
December 12th Black Diamond Hotel opened next to co-op store

1913 Bishop of Jarrow consecrated the Mission Church.
Hippodrome cinema opened by Mr. Dyson.
November 22nd United Methodist Church opened by Lord and Lady Furness.
December 13th Working Mens' Club official opening.
Hirst's charabanc service Easington to Sunderland started.

1914 **March 2nd** Infant and Junior Girls School opened.
June 20th North pit changed to big cages.

1915 **May 26th** Infant and Junior Boys School opened.
September 23rd Lamp cabin destroyed by fire.

1916 Formation of Officials Club known as The Leathercap so called because officials of the pit wore leather helmets down the pit and the miners wore cloth caps.

1917 **November 17th** Wesleyan Methodists opened.
German submarine surfaced off Hawthorn viaduct and shelled Army Camp.

1918	Influenza epidemic – very high death rate – some families lost 3 or 4 members.
1919	**December 18th** R.A.O.B. club opened at the top of school street, known as the tin club, became the Constitutional Club in 1928..
1920	Church hall opened. Primitive Methodists opened.
1921	Colliery on strike for 13 weeks.
1923	**September 1st.** Colliery cemetery opened. Catholic church opened. **September 19th** James Laidler Bell was born.
1924	**September 27th.** New road Easington to Horden opened by Mr. Gosling. M.P.
1925	Boy Scout group formed by Mr. Wilf Kirkbride. **July 11th** Aged Miners Homes opened by Peter Lee. **November 28th.** Comrades Club opened. **November 30th** Cinema started upstairs in Miners Hall.
1926	General strike. Colliery at a standstill for 30 weeks.
1927	End of back shift working.
1928	Bishop of Durham cut first sod on the site of the Church of the Ascension Constitutional Club opened on old site of R.A.O.B. club.
1929	Church of Ascension opened by Bishop of Durham on Ascension Day. **September 14th.** Foundation stone laid for Baptist church. Demolished 2009 and houses built on site. **November 14th.** Miners Hall destroyed by fire. **November 28th** Three men barred (trapped) in pit. Over 1 million tons of saleable coal produced in 1 year by 1,491 hewers and putters.

1930 **January 1st** Salvation Army Citadel (Hall) opened by British Commissioner
October 11th. I, Mary Nightingale Bell nee Duff was born.

1932 Women's Institute formed by Mrs. Oswald and Mrs. Lovelace with 35 members.

1933 **June.** Main coal seam closed down – many families leave colliery.

1934 **February 3rd.** Welfare Hall opened by T. Lishman – colliery manager.

1935 Greyhound track opened by Frank E. Franks at Easington Village.
Army drill hall built at Easington Village.
Rialto cinema opened. First picture shown – The Life of The Bengal Lancers.
December. Main coal seam reopened.

1936 **January 15th.** West Hika ran aground at Beacon Hill. More of this later.
August. Summer camp at Hawthorn Towers visited by the Duke of York.

1937 **February 20th.** Pit head baths opened.

1938 **May 14th.** Sherburn Hill store Seaside Lane destroyed by fire.
September 1st Easington secondary Modern school opened behind Glebe Terrace.

1939 **January 14th** Junior Boys school clock erected on outside of building paid for by money left over from 1937 Coronation festivities.
April 26th. British Legion Club opened.
September 3rd. War is declared.
Royal Berkshire Regiment billeted in Church hall and in Welfare hall

1940 **August 15th** Bombing of East and colliery sidings. 8 people killed, others injured and homeless.

A Chronicle of Easington Colliery

1941 — **December 24th.** North pit cage went amain down the shaft.

1942 — **April 27th** Empire cinema destroyed by fire.

1944 — **January.** One week strike – wage dispute.
March. Putters go slow. 450 putters involved.
November 9th. Jobling and Smith barred (trapped) in.
Organ from Hippodrome put into Church of Ascension.

1945 — Dennis Donnini was awarded the Victoria Cross posthumously.
May 8th 3 p.m. War in Europe is ended/ Sirens (buzzers) hooted. Bunting was no coupons. All material had been on coupons during the war.
June 8th Victory E. Day celebrated by holding street parties.
August 15th . V. J. day War with Japan over.

1947 — Public clock on school fitted with new dials and pointers.

1948 — **January 25th** Special service broad cast from Church of the Ascension.

1949 — **January 16th.** V . Brenkley., G. Elliott, J. Jackson accidentally drowned at sea off coast of Easington Colliery. All local young men.

1950 — Main coal seam permanently closed.

1951 — **May 29th Explosion in High Main Seam known as the Duckbills. 83 lives lost.**

1952 — **March 22nd** Opening of Memorial Avenue in Welfare grounds. 83 trees planted – one for each life lost- stone from disaster site set up as a monument.

1953 — **May 29th** Opening of garden of Remembrance in Colliery cemetery.

1954 — **April 24th** Colliery medical centre opened

1955 — Estimated amount of colliery waste on foreshore – ten million tons.

1956 Public band changed over and became colliery band. Welfare Bowls team were winners of Veterans League.

1957 Epidemic of Asian Influenza- many people seriously ill – some deaths.

1958 **January 4th** south pit accident – 14 men injured.
August 7th Hunters place – 9 bungalows built by Aged Miners Association opened by Manny Shinwell M.P.

1959 **October 9th** Branch Library opened in new building. Seaside Lane.
Colliery band won N.C.B. Durham area contest.

1960 N.C.B. start to put Bathrooms in colliery houses.
Petwell Estate -49 bungalows for aged people built by council.
Amateur swimming club run by Mr. and Mrs. Blackburn and W. Scott since 1948, closed. Over 500 children had been taught to swim.

1961 **December 26th** Charles Dedman accidentally killed on pit heap.

1962 **October 12th** Revival of Colliery Jazz band with A. Pratt, B.Wheatman and Melvyn Nicholson as officials The Tip Toppers were formed.

1963 Colliery band won Daily Herald Championship award.
May 4th Railway Station closed for passenger service

1964 **May 24th** Working Men's Club destroyed by fire.
July 18th R.A.F.A. club opened.
November 27th Fire in pit – 2nd South Low Main.

1965 **November 10th** Easington Colliery's oldest resident died. Mrs. Mary Martin aged 102 years.
Welfare Cricket Club win Oswald Cup.

1966 Working Men's Club partly reopened.

1967 G. Hancock accidentally killed down mine.
July 14th official opening of Working man's Club.

1968 Revival of old game of quoits. Social clubs and Public Houses make up teams and a league is formed.

1969 **July 18**th W.R. Challoner and R. Fenwick lost their lives in a pit accident on eve before Durham Big Meeting Day.
R. Mills won cup for best individual Quoit player. Central club runners up tp champions in Quoit Leagus.

1984-1985 year long pit strike.

1993 **Pit closed**

1999 R.A.F.A. club closed Black Diamond Hotel closed, British Legion closed.

Many shops began closing, some colliery houses were demolished, private houses built.

Everything began to change.

CHAPTER 1

LIFE IN EASINGTON COLLIERY

I am writing this on 10th April 1999. I think it must be very exciting to hear from someone of 100 years ago. I am 68 years old. I will be 69 before I finish this. It is to be a very (I hope) interesting story of people who lived in Easington Colliery. When you read the enclosed story it will give you an insight as to how we lived worked and thought.

At the moment we are going through a very trying time. Everything is changing. I am sure the school I have referred to will have been demolished. It is situated in Seaside Lane. It is still there, derelict in 2013. Perhaps the name Easington Colliery will have been changed to something more picturesque like Easington on Sea. Still called Easington in 2013.

The currency has already changed once in my lifetime and may be changing again.

The weather today is bright, sunny, with the occasional shower and a breeze that often blows in from the North Sea. From March winds we have April showers that will bring forth May flowers.

Happy reading

My husband Jim's family came to Easington from Haswell in about the year 1912.

The family were James (Jim's grandfather), Ann Alice (his grandmother), and three brothers James Charles and Simon. They lived in Abbot Street which was opposite the pit .They came here because the pit was just opening and they were all miners. Jim's mother lived at Sunderland and they told us when they met, Jim's father would walk to Sunderland and then back to spend time with Margaret Agnes nee MacLaughlan.

BELL. - To Margaret Agnes of Sunderland and James of Easington Colliery a baby boy James Laidler was born on September 19th 1923 at their home in the Block Houses, (top house Londonderry Terrace). Is it still here in the year 2100 ? At the moment these houses are selling at about £20,000. Probably built for £100.

The Bell's home consisted of two small rooms in this terraced house. Housing was scarce and the coalowners were having houses built specially for their workers. A lot of people at this time rented rooms out and took in single men as lodgers. A lot of people had rooms at Easington Village first, waiting for rooms or a house in the colliery area as it was closer to the pit and saved the men having a long walk to work and most importantly a long walk back after a long hard shift down the pit. The men were called pitmen; later on it was more fashionable to call them miners. The house in Londonderry Terrace had no bathroom, no hot water and an outside toilet which was shared with the other family who lived in the other rooms of the house.

James Laidler's name was shortened to Jim. When he was born he already had two older sisters, Violet and Ann. Jim's father was a miner. When Jim was nine months old the family moved to a colliery owned house, which had two bedrooms upstairs, downstairs there were two rooms, one a living room which had a big black range for cooking by coal and where the family ate too. This was the main room of the house. The other downstairs room was a small scullery with a set pot, i. e. a small boiler in which water could be heated by coal of course and then run through a tap into a bath which was also in this small scullery. When the bath was not in use it was covered by a bench which was a worktop for cooking and scrubbing the weekly wash on. The whites of the weekly wash were put in the set pot and boiled. Margaret was very proud of how white she washed the family clothes.

There was a yellow stone sink in the scullery with one cold tap; this was the only sink and the only tap with running water in the house. The set pot was filled from this tap by the bucketful. Off the scullery was a good sized pantry. The Bells were the first family to move into this estate of colliery houses called Wembley. The address was 20, John Street. situated opposite the cemetery. These houses were 'free' i.e. they were part of the miners wage and were much sought after. Any married miner not living in a colliery house got 5 shillings added to his pay. Today's money in 1999 that is 25 p The wages of pitmen was below the poverty line.

Nine months after moving into the colliery house Margaret gave birth to a fourth child Irene and she of course was eighteen months younger than Jim.

When Jim was two years old he was very ill with pneumonia and Margaret was nursing him and crying over him, fearing he was dying, a knock was heard at the door. Margaret answered it, tears in her eyes and cradling toddler Jim in her arms. A gypsy woman stood there and she asked, 'My dear, why are you crying?' Margaret replied, 'He is my only son, I am afraid I am going to loose him'. The gypsy replied, 'Don't cry over him, he will recover have a long life and will be the first child to make you a grandmother'. Jim recovered and was just like any other toddler, full of mischief. He wore his shoes out very quickly being a very active child.

Margaret tried to help the family budget by washing for her mother-in-law. Her pay, sixpence and an old loaf for doing a weeks washing. An old loaf was one baked on a Saturday and not eaten by the Monday. Mrs. Bell senior was such a 'good living' woman she did not bake on a Sunday. Margaret did the weekly wash using a poss tub - a small dust bin like tub filled with soapy water and by using a poss stick pounded the steeped clothes. In mother-in-laws household were herself and husband and two sons working at the pit so washing and ironing was quite a feat and Margaret did this for sixpence and an old loaf. The clothes the men wore down the pit were also washed at home.

One day as she was doing the weekly wash at her mother-in-laws Margaret had to tie Jim in a chair as she could not afford to buy shoes for him. His grandfather to keep him occupied poured three hundred gold sovereigns on to the table for Jim to play with. Picture now Jim at about two and a half years old - shoeless and playing with three hundred gold sovereigns

CHAPTER TWO

From now on I will call Jim's father James. In 1921 there was a pit strike throughout the country. Miners wanted a fair wage and better working conditions. This was before Jim was born. When he was three years old there was a much longer strike which lasted six months. Miners went back to work worse off. James had an allotment i.e. a very large garden away from the house in which he could grow vegetables and keep livestock. During the 1926 strike he grew vegetables and sold them. Margaret washed and ironed other peoples' laundry for coppers. She became an expert cook and baked pies, bread, cakes and scones and sold them. Nothing was ever wasted. Old coats and jumpers and suits were washed, cut into strips and made into proggy mats. The only floor covering was the mats Margaret made She made and sold them too, sitting in the oil lamplight far into the night to complete them as quickly as possible. Come to think of it the Bells were poor before and after the strike as well as during it.

The cobblers' shop was a hut on wasteland between Londonderry Terrace and the bungalows. Are they still there I wonder. The cobblers hut was demolished before the bungalows were built. Probably during the Second World War. Clothing and feeding the family on the menial miners pay was not easy and James soled and heeled the family's shoes. Jim was always wearing holes in the soles of his shoes and James patiently cobbled them. One day the stitching gave way down the back of his only pair of shoes. Margaret sent Jim to the cobblers to have them sewn. James did not have the equipment to do this. They were to be ready that evening.. Jim was sent by his mother with the coppers to collect them. Alas Mr. Shawley, the cobbler, had soled them and would not hand them over to Jim as he had insufficient money. He went home to tell his mother, Margaret went to the cobblers to sought this business out. It seemed the cobbler thought Jim had said 'These shoes are to be soled', and he had said 'These shoes are to be sowed'! Not the best of English grammar and easily misinterpreted. The cobbler was adamant it was not his mistake and he was not going to be out of pocket because of a little boys' bad grammar. He refused to hand over the shoes.

It looked as though Jim was to remain barefoot. Margaret in desperation went to plead with the cobbler's wife about her plight. She explained the misunderstanding. Mrs. Shawley handed the shoes over for the price of stitching them so Jim was shod once again.

Margaret wanted one of her daughters to go to the butchers' one day. They said "Let him go for a change, he gets away with doing nothing". Jim went for a pound of sausage his mother needed for the next meal. He loved to go to the pork butchers shop with its sawdust covered floor and great sides of meat hanging from big hooks attached to the ceiling. No strict hygiene regulations that we have today (1999) then. Also there was also the delicious smell of onions ready to go into the pork dips they sold. Pork dips were a bread bun dipped in pork fat and filled with pork and onions. Jim paid for the pound of sausages and took them home. Margaret asked him for the change and he said the butcher gave him none. Margaret was a bit puzzled, beef sausage should not have cost that much. When Margaret opened the package she bounced the sausage off young Jim's head. He had bought thick, chunky (and also very delicious) pork sausage. Fewer links to the pound in weight and also fewer to the pence. The thin beef sausage stretched further to serve the family, after picking the sausage up Margaret washed it and made a meal for the family. The sisters ran the errands after that.

Margaret occasionally recalled the gypsy's words which she often found a comfort as when Jim started school he was found in a routine medical examination to have a heart murmur. He was ordered not to partake in any athletic activities. No games was punishment indeed for this very active boisterous child. He ignored the ban and Margaret's heart missed a beat many a time as the energetic, sturdy looking, although having a heart defect Jim, jumped the three and a half foot gate leading from the back yard instead of bothering to open it.

Again and again she recalled the words forecast to her when he was a toddler. Not long after Jim started school Margaret gave birth to yet another daughter. So before Jim was seven years old he had two older sisters, Violet and Ann and two younger sisters, Irene and Hilda. A precious only son. Margaret tried to put the thought from her mind that there was a very slim chance of Jim becoming the first to make her a grandmother considering he had four sisters. It was usual for the girls to marry younger than the boys in those days, and with this reflection, if the gypsy was wrong in one thing - she could not bear the thought -.

CHAPTER THREE

In 1930 when Jim was about seven years old there was very little money coming into the Bell household, his father was on the means test. The Means Test was the checking of a persons' wage to see if they would qualify for financial aid, if you did you were very hard up. This was the smallest wage that anyone could get. Jim's father was employed at the pit but the pits at this time were frequently 'laid idle' and only worked one or two days a week. One day his mother was crying and when Jim asked her in his innocence "What is the matter", she opened her clenched fist to show him the money in it and then turned her hand over and banged it down on the table. "That's what I am crying for, twenty six shillings to keep two grown ups and five children on".

Christmas time was not a time for rejoicing because it only brought home to Margaret how poor they were. One Christmas she heard of a scheme for making money. This was by taking orders for goods for Christmas from a catalogue from friends and neighbours and in payment from the firm she collected for she would receive toys and gifts. Margaret took orders, collected the money and sent it to the suppliers. Eagerly the family awaited the arrival of the huge parcel to see what was in it for them. A tea chest arrived; Margaret carefully unpacked it and checked each item off for her neighbours against her list. All agog and wondering what her 'commission' would be. Finally she reached the end of the list - one parcel was left. Margaret opened it - very disappointed - a small oval tin filled with half a pound of sweets and a silver coloured toy pistol was her 'commission'. The pistol was Jim's only toy that Christmas.

Another Christmas his present was a cardboard Red Indian figure and a bow and a stick with a sucker on the end. He became a crack shot at hitting the Indian target.

Jim joined the Good Templars and received a Christmas gift from them The Good Templars was an organisation who met regularly for meetings and social occasions. Men, women and children were all encouraged to become members; the only condition was they signed the pledge, which meant they had never to drink alcohol. This was no hardship to a child, the officials were very devoted people and arranged parties and outings for their members. The outings were to Easington beach with sandwiches supplied.

From Sunday school he received sweets and an apple and orange. Sunday school took place in all the religious buildings. The teachers were ordinary Easington people who were interested in the moral and religious welfare of the young and hoped to help guide them on a sin free path through life at the same time teaching them the gospels.

In the summer children went on trips to the seaside. I will explain more fully about Sunday school in my own life which eventually intertwines with Jim's.

Despite the lack of money there were many happy occasions. He was a friendly little boy who made friends easily and a particular friend of his was Ernie Mills. Jim was very often to be found at the Mills' home which was four streets away from his own home. The two little boys did not need toys to play with but went exploring in the nearby quarries and denes. Unfortunately one day Ernie went to play in a quarry without Jim and never returned. When his pet dog, which never left his side, arrived home without him, his father went in search of him and was led by the dog to the quarry. Ernie had been digging a tunnel and it caved in. He was buried alive, suffocated. Mr. Bill Scott and Ernie's' father dug him out. Mr. Scott used a gripe to help dig him out, this pierced his head behind his ear.

The pit at this time in the nineteen thirties was working two or three shifts a week at the most and Jim watched his dad stand at the front door ready for work dressed in his pit clothes. . No pit head baths for the miners in those days. Another task Margaret had was every day that James worked he came home in his pit clothes -jacket, cap and trousers impregnated with the smell and dirt of the pit -she had to 'dash' these, i.e. beat them against 'off' the back yard wall to get the pit dust and as much stink of the pit off them as she could. Clothes worn down the pit could never be worn at any time other than at the pit.

If the pit buzzer did not sound James went to the pit, if the buzzer blew, down-hearted he would take his pit clothes off and go and tend his vegetables which he grew in his nearby allotment, to help feed his growing family.

There were no televisions in those days and although there were wirelesses (radios) the Bells' could not afford such a luxury. In fact there was no electricity in this house and it was Jims' job to go for the paraffin to the shop in Seaside Lane owned by Tot Williams. Margaret thought Jim should not hop, skip and jump as he carried the can of paraffin home, she did try to slow him down - never able to forget this healthy looking boisterous son had this weakness, a heart murmur.

At bedtime the children held lighted candles to see their way to bed. Jim was afraid of the dark as in his imagination he was sure weird shapes danced around the bedroom at night. The moonlight streaming in the window gave this effect. He would not go upstairs before his sisters. They tormented him about his fear but he didn't care as long as he was not first up the stairs.

CHAPTER FOUR

James decided about this time to keep pigs on his allotment. Nothing was wasted in the Bell household and the pigs could be fed on discarded vegetable peelings. Not only would he have meat and bacon for his own family he would be able to supply other families and to make a little money to eke out his pit wage.

The routine of buying piglets was to borrow Mr. Risby's (the local pig killer) pony and trap and go to Haswell mart or a farm at Easington Village to buy them. Margaret kept Jim away from school as she thought that what he could learn from his father would be more useful than any lessons to be learned in the classroom. Jim loved to take the reins of the pony and trot it along the country lanes. The three R's i.e. reading, writing, (a)rithmetic, were the main things taught at school in those days.

In 1998 I met Miss Underwood who had taught at Easington Colliery School in the nineteen thirties, she was over ninety years of age and she told me the aim of the school at that time was to make sure every pupil was literate and this was achieved in ninety nine per cent of scholars. A truly high figure showing the devotion and skill of the teachers. Jim was not so good at reading and writing. He was better at arithmetic because he learned all about money at the mart, bargaining and from listening to his mother calculating on how to make ends meet. Jim preferred the outdoor life and learned of botany and nature and the animals and birds in the fields and local lanes and denes.

Jim acquired another job at this time, that was taking his barrow and calling at houses for peelings, crusts and leftovers to feed the pigs. He called the people customers as he sold to them cabbages, lettuce and any other vegetables that could be spared from the allotment. No wonder young Jim was good at arithmetic, he learned it in the back streets not at school. So he did his share of earning at a very early age. When the pigs were ready for slaughter Jim used to take a notebook on his rounds and accept orders for pork, black pudding, pigs cheek, potted meat and all things that could be made by Margaret from a pig. He even had a customer for the trotters and tail.

It was a great day when a pig was 'knocked down' - which was the expression for slaughtering. The pigs were killed in the allotment by Mr. Risby the Pig Killer - what a title. The pigs were stunned with the flat head of a hammer and then when they were lying down, the sharp end of the hammer was put into their brain which killed them. Later on the humane killer was used, that was a steel needle fired into the brain and this was withdrawn by the same gun, later still a bullet was used. After slaughter the pigs were wheeled quickly down to the Bells' backyard, one at a time in a big barrow. All the neighbourhood children used to sit on the wall to watch Mr. Risby bloody, gutting the pigs. Jim charged them for watching this gory spectacle. Cigarette cards or marbles was the payment. They watched as the pigs' throat was cut and Margaret catching the blood in a white enamel bucket and swiftly stirring it with her bare hands and taking out clots and then by adding barley and maybe a secret ingredient, she cooked it in large tins in the oven. This was very tasty and very popular. Jim waited patiently for the bladder to use it for a football.

The weather in Jim's memory always seemed to be fine and pleasant in his young days,

The pigs' carcasses were hung up on big hooks suspended from the ceiling in the scullery over the bath to drain till they were ready for cutting up. After Margaret had made all the various meaty things and the pigs were cut up into joints Jim went to his customers and supplied them with their orders. Margaret carefully saved some of the money to buy six piglets. The rest of the profit went to buying clothes and other necessities. This cycle went on for six years.

Jim continued to attend school. Electricity was installed in the houses and the Bells' had another son, Reg. Jim was thirteen years old now. He got free milk at school every day, this was routine for large families as they were most in need, it also applied to children with a health problem, so Jim qualified on two counts. Jim went to a school summer camp for a holiday. This was arranged again for the children of big and/or needy families through the education authority. The camp was at Marsden. They were all boys. They slept in long wooden huts and slept in metal bunk beds, had good meals. When they first arrived they were all given a large pot of Senna Pod tea.!!!! They were soon all running to the toilets. The food was good and wholesome. Walls' ice-cream bicycle visited the site, the boys lucky enough to have money bought the ice cream which was in crystal form. Weather permitting the teachers, from their school who went with them, took them into the country for nature walks or along the beach. Sometimes the teachers used to sly off for a drink of the local ale.

The door was open at each end of the huts and wild rabbits would run through and the pupils would be given sixpence for every rabbit caught, which was very few as the rabbits were much too quick. Sometimes they had a sing-song on a night and the good singers would sing for the others. On a Wednesday the parents would come through on a bus trip. Margaret was too busy washing to go but James went and was amazed at all the rabbits.

The following year Jim was picked again because of being one of a large family, this time he went to Cresswell, a little further up the coast. The boys all enjoyed it, Bobby Knapper, who later became our 'best man', Arthur Smith, Stanley Ward, Sammy Rider and others. Stanley cried his eyes out because he missed his mother so much.

Before leaving school Jim used to help one of the co-operative store drivers on his rounds. Delivering groceries and driving the big draught horses pulling the heavily laden carts he was paid by the driver in kind i.e. groceries which was very helpful to the family. Driving the pony and trap to the mart with his father as a seven year old seemed to have been an apprenticeship after all. He was offered a job at this store when he left school at fourteen years of age but his mother had to be a member of this store for him to qualify for employment there. She was not and declined to do so because of the walk to the village. Jim very reluctantly had to decline the offer, this saddened the man he helped, George Collins as he and his wife had become fond of him and he accompanied George to his home every Saturday for dinner.

CHAPTER FIVE

When Jim left school his first job was at Easington Village employed by Harry Stogdale to look after his ponies and work in his scrap yard, this job lasted for two years. During this employment Jim used to sort scrap and rags, count jam jars and glass bottles for recycling , eventually he would pay the men who had hired the horses and carts from Harry Stogdale. They travelled the streets for scrap and sold it to Harry who in turn sold it on. Time after time Jim went through jacket, coat and trouser pockets hoping he would sometime find a copper or two left in an old garment but times were too hard for anyone to leave a halfpenny in a pocket.

One day Jim felt the rustle of paper as he felt in an old trouser pocket - pulling it out in his hand he thought how the gold miners had felt when they struck gold. He counted eight pound notes, mouldy and smelling, but it was still money. What to do with it! He took it home and James thought he had stolen it. No one had seen so many pound notes together in the Bell household. Jim said 'Smell it' and of course they smelt the damp mildewed paper and knew their son was no thief, but how could anyone be so rich as to have put this in a pocket and forgot it. Margaret ever thrifty and hopeful said, 'Did you go through the other pocket in that pair of trousers', Jim in his excitement had not. He went back and searched again - this was not a dirty, old, mouldy pair of discarded trousers this was a fantasy such as one dreamed of finding at the end of a rainbow. Jim discovered four more of the same foisty pound notes. He took them home. The problem, what to do with this cache.

After much deliberation as to what would happen to it if they gave it to Harry Stogdale- would they ever see any of it again and if they gave it to the police the questions they might be asked as to where it had come from - they finally decided it must be a 'gift of God' and so they kept it.

Twelve pounds was a fortune. Jim deserved a good present from this and Margaret bought him a Raleigh sports bicycle. He was fourteen years old and to own such a bike was a dream come true. He also profited by being fitted out with a navy serge suit and a white shirt. The rest of the money was spent on sprucing up the house and family.

Next he went to work for a local farmer, Jack Mitchell at Paradise farm. Jack had a contract to deliver best coal from Easington pit throughout the area. Jim used to drive the big horses pulling heavy cartloads of best coal out of the pit yard and distribute it to colliery officials' houses as well as work in the fields.

One bitterly cold day when the north east wind was blowing bitingly across the land an officials wife Mrs. Ripley asked him if he would like something to warm him up as he must be freezing. Thinking in terms of hot tea or oxo Jim was surprised when she gave him a sandwich, she informed him it was a mustard sandwich, and it was something to warm him up indeed. He thought no wonder these people had plenty of money if they ate as sparingly as this. Mustard sandwiches- his mother always managed something better than this.

Years later in the nineteen nineties an old horse keeper who had worked at the pit looking after the pit ponies told me every time he saw Jim he remembered him as a young boy coming over snow drifts in the fields from the colliery, driving two huge shire horses in double tracers when no one else could get through the six foot drifts bringing food called choppy to the pit as they had run out of food for the ponies .He said it was the best sight he had ever seen.

The Bells' finances were looking up, not a lot, but they were improving because Violet and Ann were working too. The girls were employed doing housework for different people. Dailies they would have been called in a later age. Irene soon followed. If any of these children had the ability to go to the local grammar school they would not have been able to. The family budget could never stretch to the special uniform. The grammar school children went to school until they were sixteen, the Bell children had to leave school at fourteen.

CHAPTER SIX

When the second world war started Jim was working on the farm, Margaret was not worried about his being called up to go to war as she thought with his medical history he would never pass a medical examination to go into the forces. Jim left the farm when he was eighteen, he applied for a post as head horsekeeper and got it. Fifty applied for the job. By a strange quirk of fate this was the end of his horsy career. Jim got the job to begin a week come Monday, on the Monday following the Saturday his calling up papers arrived to go into the Royal Navy. He never got the chance to start his new position at the local co-operative store. 'Working at the store' was thought to be one of the best jobs in the area.

Jim had to attend Newcastle for a medical, Margaret accompanied him very sure he would not pass his medical because of his heart murmur. Doctors pronounced him medically fit A1. Margaret cried her eyes out because he was fit enough to go into the Royal Navy and he would be taken from her !!! Jim was travel sick journeying to Newcastle by bus but this did not deter him in his ambition to be a sailor.

His naval career had begun. Jim was ordered to report to Pthwelli in North Wales. His train did not stop at North Wales but travelled first to South Wales then circled round to North. His first time aboard a train and this journey lasted nineteen hours.

On alighting at Pthwelli railway station on a wet dark October night he finally arrived at H.M.S. Glendower. This was the name of the training ship. Jim reached the training camp, stood in the pouring rain appalled at this awesome horrifying sight. A high wire fence surrounded the camp and the gate was guarded by naval personnel armed with rifles. He felt like a prisoner. Jim who loved the open air could have cried, he cursed under his breath at whoever had compelled him to leave home. He identified himself to the sentries and was admitted to the beginning of a new way of life. He was directed to the dining room, his first meal after all this travelling was waiting for him. He couldn't believe it. Two slices of corned beef and a few cold boiled potatoes, he never ate them and for the rest of his life could not stomach corned beef and cold potatoes. Then he sat and cried, Margaret's beloved son - not the only son as after Reg came Tom who had just been born. Although they were poor in money Jim had never been lonely before, now he was on his own. Was he still in the British Isles? Here anyone he asked the way or tried to speak to looked at him with unfriendly eyes as though he was a foreigner and couldn't understand his north eastern accent and asked him to speak slower and still looked at him blankly. Here he was, alone and far from the pit village of Easington Colliery which had been his whole world where everyone knew each neighbour, every face was familiar. Heated by open coal fires every house was as warm as the people. Would his family know where he was? When would he see Easington again – ever?

The training for action at war lasted three months and began by being issued with uniform, hammock and bedding, a 'housewife' which was a cloth folded up containing needles, cotton and wool for sewing and darning, something only females ever did, he had seen his mother often enough mending torn and worn clothes. He was going to have to learn how to sew. He was given a kit bag to pack everything into. He was taught how to march, drill, how to identify ships and planes, rifle shooting and all about guns. Part of his duties was spells of guarding the cliffs of Wales. The time of the year, October, November, December 1942, the wettest, coldest and windiest winter for decades found him parading along the rugged coastline on sentry duty. The rats as big as cats ran about in the dark. The people in this part of Wales only spoke Welsh, the other sailors all seemed by their accents to belong to the southern counties and all sounded posh to Jim. His accent was unique and not understood by many. Nobody called him Jim anymore, he was nicknamed Dinger, they changed his name, changed his occupation but no one could ever change his pitmatic accent. Every one he knew came from the north and he was proud of it. Jim sent his civilian clothes home but they never arrived, clothes were rationed so they were most likely stolen. Jim learned to look after his equipment. He learned if he left anything lying about some light fingered person would pick it up. They were living in chalets and a young sailor in a neighbouring chalet hung himself. Jim thought often of his doting parents, his warm home and loving family and wondered if he would ever see them again.

Jim's next instructions were to report to Portsmouth. On arriving after a train journey shorter than the first, he queued for a meal. Someone called his name, "Ordinary Seaman Bell report to the office", he left the line waiting for a meal and presented himself. He did not get the chance to go back for that meal. Jim was informed he had been drafted to a ship and it was going to sail immediately. He asked what kind of a ship, the officer on hearing his accent told him it was a coal boat. This could well be as in his training he had been trained for the D.E.M.S. i.e. The Defence of Merchant Ships. The officer was being sarcastic and 'taking the mickey' as it was called. He was told to go straight to the docks; the ship he was drafted to was H.M.S. Blencathra, a hunt class destroyer. She was sailing immediately. Jim went post haste to the docks carrying his kit bag and the ship had sailed. No coal boat this but a fighting escort ship. Jim had trained to be a gunner. Travelling by train to Southend he caught up with the ship. Eighteen years old with three months training he was considered to be fully trained to go to sea to fight against the Germans. The ship was based at Sheerness. H.M.S. Blencathra was ordered to patrol the English Channel.

On one occasion Blencathra escorted ships to the river, Motor Launches and Motor Torpedo Boats and an old destroyer, Lord Louis Mountbatten's first ship, The Campletown. The target was the lock gates at Dieppe, the Blencathra could not go up the river as it was too big to turn round in a hurry in the river. The M.L.'s and the M.T.B's were able to; they were going to bring the crew of the Campletown back to England if all went well. The Blencathra was guarding the mouth of the river and standing by for who knows what. The lock gates were to be rammed by the old destroyer so that the Germans could not use the dry dock. The campaign was a great success with unfortunately a great loss of life. They were also trying to free the Free French. More than fifty years later Jim was to receive from the Free French a certificate thanking him for his part in the attack and a medal.

About this time Knocker (Norman White), a signalman wrote this account which shows that there were some occasional entertaining times amongst the crew.

"In 1941 & 1942 we used to go to Southend-on-Sea to pick up convoys and take them up the east coast or through the straits of Dover which was a very hazardous area 24 hours a day. Sometimes we had to wait overnight for a convoy to form up in to position, so occasionally, no I should say very occasionally if you were in the liberty watch you could go ashore and enjoy sleeping in a proper bed. The snag was you had to catch the pier train for the one and a quarter mile journey to the pier head where we joined our motor boat. Of course I had to miss the train once (you never did it twice) and had to run the full one and a quarter miles. The motor boat had just left but fortunately the coxswain saw me waving or heard me yelling, or both, and came back to pick me up. I expect that was a day when my tot (every sailor in the Royal Navy received a tot of rum a day) would have gone down the throats of the motor boat operator - either Dinger - Jim Bell or Queenie - Bill Hanson. He got that nickname as he was born in Queen Street, Pompey, as Portsmouth was known then.

On another occasion a certain nameless communication person got into the carriage and suddenly produced two gigantic pairs of A.T.S. passion killers (women's army knickers). You can imagine that trip to Blencathra was somewhat noisier and happier than usual when returning to duty. On arrival out of the motorboat, across the gangway, top speed to the Signal Bridge and up went the 'trophies' on the starboard halyards. Suddenly Yeoman Robson sees the 'Signal', goes purple and starts yelling at everyone. He rushes to pull down the 'signal' informing us of our fate if Captain D21 saw it. He threatened all sorts of punishment, but he never followed it up. I do not think he even thought the culprit was one of Jock Melroses' boys. He made a real 'bloomer.' Lighter moments aboard the Blencathra. Jock Melrose was the Chief Yeoman. The liberty watch was the off duty time.

This report appeared during that time in a south country newspaper headlines.

'Hundredth Convoy - Blencathra always dodges the shells, the account continued - In the wardroom of the hunt class destroyer H.M.S. Blencathra, Lieutenant Sidney Parkhouse D.S.O.R.N. her engineer officer recently had a special celebration of his own. Her engine had just completed 30,000,000 revolutions without an involuntary stop or a single breakdown. Blencathra has completed her hundredth channel convoy. "I should think she has been shelled by the German guns more times than any other war ship", said Lt. Parkhouse "But they have not hit her yet, though once or twice they were close" A short time ago Blencathra was in action against four U - boats but she claims no more than to have done some damage.

This account summarises Jim's first six months aboard the Blencathra. He was one of the gunners who defended the channel and fired on the U-boats. Day was night. Night was day. During the war whatever the time or day the Blencathra was on the alert for action. Meals were eaten when you could and if you could spare the time. Jim's thoughts when not occupied fighting the damned war pondered on his family and friends in Easington Colliery. They would never believe this was happening to him. Things were more severe and dramatic than anything happening at the local picture houses, The Rialto, Hippodrome and The Empire. It was hard to imagine life must be going on as usual in his home village. How long would the war go on? He doubted that he would survive.

The captain summoned the crew to muster on the upper deck and he said "Take a good look at the shore, I don't suppose you will see this for a long time!". He then explained what they were going to do.

H.M.S. Blencathra had been ordered to leave the channel and the next duty began. She sailed from Sheerness up the east coast. As the ship was passing off the coast of Easington Jim trained the binoculars on it and an officer said "Is there something interesting out there". "Yes that is where I live and that is the pit" he replied, noting a new engine house had just been built. The officer replied "Take a long look it will be a long time before you see it again". He didn't think at the time it would be three years before he saw it again. Sailing round Scotland they refueled in Ireland. There she joined a convoy and set sail for the Atlantic The Blen's job was as escort and protector and had to work much as a wagon leader did in the wild west rounding his wagons up, helping any in trouble, continuously riding up and down, round and round the convoy chasing and protecting as though a shepherd, any straggler.

In a stormy mid Atlantic this convoy was joined by a convoy of American ships. Their destination was the Mediterranean Sea. There were 1,500 ships in this convoy by this time. The largest convoy of the war to ever sail up to this time and was gathering to sail for the Invasion of Sicily. This was reported by a B.B.C. correspondent on board the Blencathra as 'being the biggest naval pageant of the war. The sea was covered with ships as far as the eye could see, they came from every allied port in the Med. as well as the huge convoy escorted by the Blencathra. The ships were of all sizes battleships, liners, tramps and motor launches, if it was seaworthy it was there, fast or slow. Hundreds and hundreds of ships". By zero hour 2.45a.m. (did day or night matter) all the ships were positioned, it was a Saturday, 10th July, strange the things that stick in one's mind. Some of the ships had landing craft aboard as well as infantry and tanks.

Heavy seas were running and half a gale was blowing. The Blen's destination was the southern tip of Sicily, their job to go close inshore and bombard the gun batteries and beaches and cover the grounding of the landing craft. Now the Blen was an attacker as well as a protector. The weather suddenly moderated, it seemed like a miracle. No doubt most of the sailors felt as though their prayers were answered. It was enough having to fight the enemy without having to fight the elements as well. They approached the land under ideal conditions. All through the long seemingly unendless night aircraft droned overhead carrying paratroops and towing gliders with shock troops - the famous Red Devils.

At about midnight the deep blue velvet like sky was studded with stars glittering like diamonds H.M.S. Blencathra was creeping silently and smoothly through the now calm water, unobserved and was now within point blank range of the shore batteries. Suddenly Jim from his position behind his Oerlikon gun saw lots of red lights bobbing in the water. The thought crossed his mind, are we nearer land than we think, then through the still air cries floated in the darkness. The bobbing red lights were attached to men whose glider had crashed into the sea, they were shouting thinking they may be run down by one of the many ships, some of the men were still clinging to the glider. The men, thinking the Blen could be a foreign ship and fearing they were going to be left or perhaps could not all be seen were shouting 'Here we are. Don't leave us'. The rescue crew picked them up, Jim was watching from the upper deck. The survivors were hauled aboard with ropes dropped over the side. When the glider had crashed it had immediately submerged and the paratroopers had to cut their way through the fabric underwater. All but one, a twenty year old got out. As soon as the airmen were on board two sergeants began shouting at each other and fighting. A strange sight this, two Englishmen fighting aboard a British destroyer - all waiting to attack the enemy. No doubt they were frustrated at not being able to complete their mission successfully. The men were calmed down and taken down below to be dried off. They thanked God for the navy. Apparently the young man who did not survive had tried to cut his way out of the top of the glider; the way to safety was through the side.

The stillness was uncanny, coloured flares floated above and then plunged from the now moonless sky. There was an occasional burst of gunfire from the shore. It was zero hour for the landing, shadowy forms alongside the Blen could be seen stealing silently towards the beach, these were the landing craft with tanks and troopships filled with Monty's army. Jim and the rest of the gunners were stripped for action and ready to open fire, suddenly signals from shore said the airborne troops and the landing craft troops had been successful and the covering fire was unnecessary. The surprise had been complete on land and sea - not a single shot had been fired as this vast fleet had crept near the shore. Then the action began - another great convoy of ships arrived, together they closed in on the island of Sicily and bombarded inland points. Dawn broke over an amazing scene. The black smoke from fires, a background for the orange flashes of gunfire could be seen as the sun shone relentlessly in the cloudless sky. The thunder like noise from the guns was deafening. Swarms of troops continued to land backed up by the R.N. The destroyers were circling the liners and supply ships, firing continuously, protecting them from the now alert enemy. The Blen then went closer inshore to protect other shipping from air attacks. The troopers passing on the last landing barge cheered and waved to the Blencathra. The beaches were crowded with men, guns, tanks and supplies moving inland to make room for more. From far inland came the occasional burst of gunfire and heavy explosions.

As the pattern of resistance became clear, it was round Pazzallo that it seemed to be strong. The Blen was ordered to bombard Pazzallo that night. Picture the scene at 9.30pm, gun flashes could be seen lighting up the dark sky. It looked at one time as though the sky was on fire, the whole ship reeked of cordite smoke. The guns continued firing and then a huge explosion was heard from and seen on the land, a big fire started in the target area. The Blen was carrying out orders admirably.

Then came the first air attack. The Luftwaffe had arrived (the German air force). From every ship red tracers were flying into the air. The night sky was flashing with explosions and as aircraft were shot down they appeared to be like giant fireworks exploding then falling into the sea. Continuously firing at aircraft and bombarding the shore four more times that night the enemy attack gradually ceased. The signal came from the shore, "A number of enemy troops wish to surrender", Pazzallo had surrendered. The city was handed over to the army.

Admiral Ramsay's order of the day to the Blencathra had been "You must continually bear in mind that the army are helpless and entirely dependent upon us until we establish them on shore. We did not let them down when they retreated from Dunkirk, in Greece and Crete and we will not let them down now when they are advancing. We have this inestimable advantage on this occasion of being associated with the veteran troops of the Eighth Army and with the Canadian and U.S. army. We have overwhelming strength in the air and are on the crest of a wave while our enemies are in the trough. We have the opportunity now to hasten their downfall. I count therefore on every man doing his utmost. Good luck and Godspeed."

The order of the day had been well and truly carried out. How many miles or waves or seas or light years from Easington? Would he ever see it again?

CHAPTER SEVEN

The days were long and the temperature was scorching. The heat of the day was almost unbearable. The nights in extreme were freezing cold. Jim, some days and nights had no time to think of the climate. Seas were stormy at times and winds were gale force but the Mediterranean bases had to be guarded - the seas to be patrolled, this was the duty of the Blen, based in Malta she escorted convoys to and for constantly and continuously threatened by enemy planes she rounded up her convoys and guarded them like a loving shepherd.

One day as Jim was walking along the upper deck to enter the canteen flat to go down below he had to step over the Petty Officer to go down to the mess deck he noticed he was checking the hand grenades He said to the officer "You've got one there without a pin in" and he threw it over the side immediately and when Jim and the P.O. realised what had happened Jim later said, "I think the both of us broke into a sweat. I never said anything else I just carried on. The P. O. was a gunnery officer and it was part of his job to check and inspect the ammunition for safety".

Forty years later at a reunion of destroyer crews Chief petty Officer Stoker Pollard told me how Jim had shot a Messerschmitt 109 (German fighter plane) down. He asked who had shot the plane down and recommended Jim for Mention in Dispatches. Captain Warren, the first commander Jim served under also said at the same reunion that he often 'wondered what the young sailors thought of me at that time when I was pushing them almost beyond human endurance'. I told him Jim had told me he thought he was coloured, he said he thought Jim was coloured too. Of course all the crew were very tanned with the sun that they had never been used to. Actually Jim had said to me he thought Cpt. Warren was a coloured so and so. You had to blame some one for the tortuous life, the sun and sea were altering the fair complexioned crew and seemed to be changing appearance as well as their characters with these horrific experiences of death and destruction of war

The ship patrolled off the beaches of Salerno and Anzio for the next six weeks never going ashore. The Blencathra was refueled from the big ships. Her guns bombarded the coast to stop the Germans from landing. Jim learned to sleep standing up, he wedged himself in a 45 degree angled corner of the Oerlikon gun deck, and if there was any action he would be immediately alert as the earphones were always in his ears. Shipmate John Seldon who was Jim's messenger i.e. bosuns' mate, Jim was the bosun, recalled the places they had slept in when they could. Did I say sleep, cat napped is nearer the mark- still half alert and listening and instantly ready for action and not quite twenty years old, he slept standing.

The Germans retreated from this coast and one quiet night, (the Mediterranean can be a very silent sea) everything was still and calm, the Blen was patrolling along the coast of Italy. Suddenly an E-boat came speeding astern of them. It was thought all the E-boats in this area had been captured or sunk. This one was flying the Italian flag, we were at war with Italy. A message was flashed from the bridge to the guns - if it continues to follow- open fire. The after turret obeyed the command, fired four inch shells and blew her out of the water!! A radio message from another ship- the Italian E-boat had been captured by the Americans but was still flying the Italian flag. Why?

And why did she appear to be chasing after the Blen? Did they try to play a trick on the British ship, thinking it would speed up and run away? If so they did not know much about the Royal Navy. No one would ever know. Perhaps they 'forgot' to change the flag. Whatever the reason the cost was the whole American crew who manned this E-boat. Captain Warren had to attend an enquiry about this incident. It was held aboard a large battleship in the middle of the war torn Mediterranean. The verdict - c'est la guerre - nothing else was ever heard about it.

H.M.S.Blencathra continued patrolling along the Italian coast, shells fired from the shore landed near them, sometimes too close for comfort. Then they moved further away from the land to deeper waters. One morning four soldiers known as spotters were taken on board the Blen and landed by them on the coast of Italy. The duty of the spotters was to find where the shells were coming from. The Blen patrolled backwards and forwards enticing the mysterious gunner to keep opening fire at them to enable the spotters to find their target. They did. The enemy could not resist the temptation of trying to sink the Blen. A gun was found hidden behind a wall in a church yard, this is why the Blen could not see their attacker. The spotters signalled the position of their tormentors. The skipper ordered the main armament to open up and blast the gun off the earth. The spotters signalled back whether the shots were over or below the target. Three turrets then concentrated on the target and bulls eye the hidden gun and gunmen were blown to bits. The ships gunners were congratulated again.

As Jim with some of his shipmates sat down to dinner that day corned beef and cold potatoes might have been welcome as meals were very rarely finished on this hazardous, dangerous patrol. Another signal came from the spotters, two enemy tanks were seen coming down the road and they gave the position to the Blen. Short work was made of them. The spotters who were well trained and active radioed a short while later that two recovery vehicles were on the way to the scene, the Blen flattened them too. She then picked up the spotters and made back to the convoy. The gunners congratulated the gunners on the accuracy of their shooting. Air attacks continued relentlessly and H.M.S. Warsprite got a bomb down her funnel and had to be escorted back to Malta for repairs. Once again the Blen was at hand, guarding her by fighting off the enemy air and sea attackers trying to sink the crippled ship as well as the Blen.

They came back to Salerno and had to go close in on the beach because the Hambledon had gone aground after firing at tanks running along the beach, they had got too zealous and went too near the land and the Blen had to go in stern first to drag her to safety both ships being fired on all the time and returning the fire.

Back to patrolling the beaches the skipper mustered the crew on to the upper deck to warn them of the extra danger of their next mission, they had to cross two mine fields while escorting a minelayer up the Italian coast. The Blen sailed through minefields going at top speed, that way it was reckoned the mines would not have time to damage them if they exploded!! The skipper told them to pray!! They went through the mine fields without mishap and when they had escorted the minelayer safely to its ordered position the news came Italy had surrendered. Another prayer was answered.

Four decades later Jim's sisters going through some old papers at the family home found this prayer sent to the family by Jim from the Med. It seems appropriate to include it now.

A PRAYER BEFORE BATTLE

O lord, I have no need to tell,
When last I prayed thou knowest well
Yet Father I may still call thee,
My cry will echo o'er the sea,
And will not fall on deafened ears,
Despite the passing of the years.
Understanding as thou art,
Give me strength to fill my part,
Help me now, Dear Lord I pray,
To fear not what I face today,
Give me courage to endure,
Cleanse my heart and make it pure.
Succour, comfort, be my guide,
Be thou always at my side,
Grant O Father of us all,
Thy pardon should my body fall,
That when the battle's truly won,
I shall be fit to be thy son.

This sent from a boy who had to become a man, fighter, defender and remain emotionless at not quite twenty

CHAPTER EIGHT.

Another day the Blen was patrolling alertly scanning the air and sea, they were on the look out for any enemy but particularly a mine laying schooner which they had been radioed was 'somewhere around'.

They spotted a winUboat and stopped her and sent a boarding party on to this suspicious looking foreign winUboat. U boats used this type of boat as a cover occasionally, tying up alongside them. The boarding party found nothing untoward and let her go on her way. The Blencathra carried on along the east coast to Marseilles and Toulon. A thick fog dropped over the sea, suddenly ping-ping the astic had picked a vessel up. The crew thought at last the mine laying schooner was somewhere in the pea soup fog. Jim was ready at his gun and the rest of the crew was at action stations. The fog opened slightly like a pair of curtains parting and there ahead of them was - not the mine laying schooner - but a U-boat on the surface. It quickly dived; the U-boat had obviously caught sight of the Blen as soon as there was a gap in the fog too.

Then began the long trail, the Blen belonged to the hunt class of destroyers and proved it was worthy of being a member. She followed the enemy boat for sixty miles as a pack of hounds would follow its quarry till there was a kill. They left the fog behind them sailing into a clear sky and sea. They arrived off the coast of Sicily still following their victim the u boat. At this position the Blen was joined by destroyers Tumult, Laforey and Hambledon.. The destroyers sent depth charge after depth charge into the deep sea but it seemed as though they could not reach their target. It was lying on the bottom of the sea bed.

The destroyers circled round the doomed U-boat, those on the surface knowing it was there by the astic echoes. Almost invisible it was a dot and a ping. At midnight, watches on R.N. ships are changed, at that exact moment the U-boat surfaced firing torpedoes as it did so. The Laforey was ahead of the Blencathra and she was the unlucky ship. Two torpedoes found their target in the boiler room of the Laforey. The Blen together with the other destroyers fired angrily at the U-boat - the conning tower was hit - the stern was hit, blue lights flashed from the U-boat in the midnight sky together with gold and silver flashes from the guns. Jim was as usual in his post manning his gun. From this position he could see the Germans climbing out of the conning tower, running along the deck and jumping into the water. The noise hardly noticed at the time was deafening, the air was filled with the turbulence of guns, shouting and explosions. The U-boat blew up and as she sank Jim looked forward to look at the Laforey which was only about 200 yards ahead of the Blen, it was standing on end with its bows standing straight up in the air and he watched it sliding slowly below with its charged depth charges exploding blowing the men in the water up as it went. Then orders were given to pick survivors up, British or Germans. The desperate search began; six Germans were picked up destined to be interrogated later. The Blen searched frantically but not in vain for survivors of the Laforey. Wounded, dying and dead were plucked out of the midnight sea. The dead were placed on the quarter deck then taken to the heads (a naval term for toilets). The naval surgeon was Lt. Commander Glass, an American, he and his medical team rushed from injured to dying trying to relieve pain. Life saving operations were performed on the table in the wardroom. Two sick berth attendants were the medical team, one of these an oldish man who Jim thought he would be about forty and a very gentle man, the other a young lad, the average age of the crew was about twenty five years so forty was 'oldish' then. Some of the crew went into the water and tied the wounded to bamboo stretchers, then they scrambled on board and carried those they rescued to safety below deck, Jim was in the thick of this as was to be expected rushing around as were the rest of the crew, saving men, hurrying to reach the drowning to lift them to safety. As one of the wounded strapped in a bamboo stretcher was lowered down below Jim stretched his arms out to take the weight of it , as it tipped, blood poured down Jim's face and battle stained clothing. This sailor was mortally wounded. Jim unstrapped him not realising he was dying, he asked Dr.Glass for help for this man, he gave him a phial of morphine and told him to inject him, this was the first time anyone had died in his arms. He had a hole in his back big enough to put two fists in. Jim did not even have the time to find out who he was. He made the Christian cross of Christ across his chest, said a prayer for him and then went to help the next man and the next. . One man, a Laforey survivor, climbed over the guard rail naked, his clothes blown off him, his right eye hanging down on his cheek, covered in bleeding wounds.

The battle was over but the scars it left would always be there. These sailors from all over England would never forget this action. It would be remembered by one Jim of Easington Colliery too. During that long seemingly endless night the crew only knowing it was night by the darkness on deck, cared for the wounded and the dying. One of the crew stopped Jim and said " It's about time you got your wounds seen to". The blood from the upturned stretcher that had drenched Jim in red had dried on him and one of his shipmates had presumed it was Jims'. When he realised how he looked he went into the heads to be sick, it was full of the bodies of the dead, nowhere to go for any relief.

Picture him now a twenty year old experiencing by now more than other people ever did in a lifetime. The next day and no-one knew how they managed with so little sleep, the Blen proceeded to Naples to land the prisoners and the wounded, more were to die on the journey. The sky was cloudless, the temperature red hot, the sea calm and peaceful looked as though it had been ironed over it was so smooth. No sign of the tragedy that had occurred previously. Beneath this sea was the U-boat and some of its crew. A watery unmarked grave. Beneath that same sea the crew of the Laforey who were not lucky enough to survive were also entombed. Enemies united now in death.

Volunteers were asked for to sew the dead in canvas bags, two of the lads offered their services. How many brave young men were there on this ship? Everyone. The two young valiant seamen were plied with rum by the crew, they prayed as they stitched twenty five bodies into twenty five canvas bags. The rum seemed to have no intoxicating effect during these gloomy funereal hours. Silently offering prayers heavenward for the dead, the dying and lastly themselves they sewed as quickly as they knew how, weighting each body by tying pig iron for weight on the leg, sending frequently for more from the ships' bilges.

It was time to bury the dead at sea. Jim was in charge of the prisoners, they too had lost crew mates and also their ship had been sunk. The guard rails at the side of the ship were lowered, the Blens' engines stopped. Picture now the blue Mediterranean Sea bathed in sunshine, this one small destroyer in the middle silently waiting to inter its dead into the water. Twenty five canvas coffins were laid on the upper deck containing twenty five young male bodies killed in action.

The skipper and the crew were assembled on the upper deck ready for the funeral service. Jim was ordered to bring the Germans from below, he was not able to tell them what was happening as neither he nor they were bi-lingual. The Germans marched on to the deck, as soon as they saw what was about to take place one, who had a stripe on his now dry uniform took over , shouting commands in German the young foreign sailor ordered his small party to stand at attention. Clicking their heels in true German like manner they did so. No doubt they would be thinking of their lost comrades whose coffin was a U-boat

Here was an unforgettable scene twenty five buried at sea in one day with enemies united on the deck of a British destroyer, by grief. This war, such a long way from Easington Colliery was a funny war, sinking ships and saving the crew. Is this a nightmare or a dream? Jim thought about it and knew he had never seen anything like this even on a film. The horror stayed with him for ever.

The ship sped back to Naples and landed the injured and the prisoners and more dead who had died from wounds. The Blen had no time to lower the usual gang plank, a narrow plank was stretched across from the ships' deck to jetty. The prisoners were blind folded before being brought to the upper deck. They were placed in single file, the second and so on grasping the shoulder of the man in front. When they realised they were 'walking the plank' they began shouting to each other in their foreign tongue. When the first reached terra firma he shouted louder than any of them. They quietened down, still blindfolded they were taken by American soldiers. Bundled into trucks the Americans butted them cruelly with their rifles. Jim and some of the crew shouted at the yanks telling them to cool it. He never heard of those Germans again. They must have an unforgettable experience to recall.

The bodies of the dead were respectfully and reverently taken ashore and given to the Americans who were seen as the Blen hastily went on her way throwing the bodies, which had been carefully sewn into their canvas bags, by a soldier at each end of the bag - one - two - three - throw as though they were garbage.

The deck was hosed down as soon as they sailed on there way to wash all traces of oil that had seeped from the bodies. At times Jim thought this must have been in a film, this couldn't reality, but he knew it was. He wished it wasn't. In 1999 as I write this Jim says "We were young".

The Blen sailed for its base in Malta and tied up for two days in which time the crew were allowed ashore. This was their 'rest'. Their base was changed to Alexandria and they were refuelled, and stocked up with food and ammunition once again.

CHAPTER NINE

The Blencathra next sped through the unmerciless heat of the Mediterranean to Anzio. Once again they were under heavy fire from enemy aircraft. Fighter German planes were attacking a hospital ship as one flew in to the assault it had to pass over the Ben and Jim stationed at his gun opened fire and brought the Messerchmitt 109 down... It never came out of its attacking dive, overshooting the medical ship after Jim's gun found its mark it crashed into the sea. There were no survivors from this aircraft. Jim never told me but Chief Petty Officer Pollard told me forty years later that Jim was mentioned in despatches for this. C.P.O. Pollard was chief engine room officer and greatly admired Jim's shooting ability and demonstrated to me all those years later how Jim had shot this plane down and saved the ship.

Unfortunately the hospital ship had been very badly hit by other aircraft, the crew abandoned ship and she became a hazard to shipping. The Blen was ordered to sink this hull of a ship, she would not sink. The gunners joked that they could only sink German ships and that British ships were so well made they were unsinkable. Wishful thinking.

Jim was one of the gunners firing on her and they knew through their many experiences that because she was so full of holes and so hot due to the many fires burning in her that as each shot was fired the hole filled up because of the heat. The Blen resorted to torpedoes and she sank instantly.

They proceeded to the Duodecanees Islands. They were commanded to 'sink anything you see, German transports or German merchant ships'.

One day the Blen along with two other destroyers H.M.S.Penn and Pathfinder set sail for Le Ross, one of the islands. Each destroyer carried forty tons of different kinds of ammunition on their upper decks. Le Ross was occupied by our troops. British troops had landed and taken it from the Germans. The British destroyers sped with their cargo to keep them well armed, unfortunately the Germans had taken the island back from the British when the three destroyers arrived on the scene. The ships were ordered to dump all this, forty tons per ship, ammunition in case of an air attack. Fortunately there was no air attack at that particular moment. What secrets this Mediterranean Sea has buried in it.

The orders came "Go in and bombard the island" The Penn and Pathfinder sailed in to attack the harbour followed by the Blen. The Blen turned sideways and blocked the entrance so nothing could escape.

The Blen went into battle with battle ensign flying at the mast head and the Jolly Roger flag designed with skull and crossbones flying below it. The weather was idyllic, the sea calm and friendly. Nothing on the sea was friendly. It was a wonderful sight. Jim felt his pulses racing and his blood surging excitedly. He was enjoying the kill and the thrill of battle now. The three destroyers bombarded, blasted and flattened everything and every body within range on that island. Well satisfied and with no regrets the three sister ships returned victoriously to continue patrolling the Dodecanees. Mission successfully completed.

The next patrol was just as exciting, unfortunately the Blen ran out of oil and being six hundred miles from Alexandria, their base, could not get back and dare not hang about waiting for another ship to refuel from because of the constant air attacks. Bad enough being attacked from the air when on the move without standing still. They would be a perfect unmissable target then. They sheltered in Turkish waters, neither the ship nor the planes dare fire at each other as Turkey was a neutral country. That is why the Blen had fled into Turkish waters. Turkish officials requested to be allowed on board. Permission was given , the leader of the Turks was a short, well fed looking swarthy man, who looked hostile, he left amid cat calls and hand signals from the crew as the out come was the ship was given twenty four hours to get out of their waters or the entire crew and ship would be interred for the duration of the war.

The Blen was reputed to be a lucky ship. Luck did not desert her now, a destroyer came stealthily along side in the dark stillness of the starless night and gave half her fuel to the Blen. They both slid out of Turkish waters no doubt to the relief of the officials of Turkey.

Back to Alexandria to be restocked, refuelled and rearmed then on to another patrol. While they were vigilantly doing their policing of the sea they were ordered to go to the aid of two destroyers. one was badly hit and disabled after a skirmish, she was H.M.S.Rockwood. The Blen was ordered to tow her back to Alex. She did this travelling at seventeen knots, too fast but air attack was imminent and U-boats were reported to be heading for this area. No time to hang about with a crippled ship in tow. The Blen with its 'passenger' had to get out quick. The steel hawser used for towing snapped so her anchor chain was used as a tow rope. These two ships together like this were sitting ducks.

This is an account sent to me by Commander Warren in command of H.M.S.Blencathra at this time.

SUMMARY OF THE AEGEAN OPERATION 1943/44

This operation had political overtones. It was instigated by Winston Churchill in an endeavour to lure Turkey into the war on the side of the allies; however, America did not go along with the idea and refused to release aircraft or give assistance to cover the British naval and military forces involved. As for Germany their forces occupied and fortified many of the larger islands in the Aegean and Rhodes provided an excellent air base from which to cover their own forces and attack ours. British forces were thereby deprived of adequate air protection and in consequence, this operation cost the loss of seven destroyers and five cruisers severely damaged with heavy casualities.

TOWING OF H.M.S.ROCKWOOD

H.M.S. Rockwood had been damaged by a glider/propelled missile fired from an aircraft in the night. She had been towed by one of the other destroyers in company into Turkish, territorial waters and anchored.

TOWING OPERATION.

H.M.S. Blencathra was instructed by C. in C. Eastern Med to render Rockwood every assistance and to tow her to Alexandria after completing her patrol in the area. Under cover of darkness, Blencathra entered Turkish territorial waters to rendezvous with Rockwood. Rockwood on the other hand had made excellent preparations whilst waiting and had made ready eleven and a half shackles of her anchor cable as the towing link between the two ships, and so with very little delay, towing commenced and because of the extra strength of the cable over conventional wire, speed could be increased and so reduce the time the ships would be in the area of the Aegean with the risk of air attacks. Speeds of 14/15 knots were reached under ideal weather conditions. However, when subsequently we were ordered to report our position, course and speed, the C. in C. replied that he considered our speed was excessive. Perhaps if I had been in Alexandria at the time I might have agreed, but under the circumstances, I was prepared to be a little more venturesome - the risk paid off !

It was therefore with God's providence and good fortune that the mission was successfully carried out.

note: twelve and a half shackles of cable = 862ft. approx. or 300 yards.

This report is signed by E.G.Warren who also sent us pictures of H.M.S.Rockwood being towed by the anchor chain of the Blen. That was the official version.

The two ships skidded across the Med at top speed and arrived safely home. Home now was Alexandria not Easington Colliery. Another mission successfully completed

CHAPTER TEN

Convoy duties continued, Blencathra patrolled the Med. methodically and meticulously but the days and nights were never monotonous. The ships duties were to take materials, ammunition, food and stores of all kinds to different ports in this brilliant blue with unbearable temperatures, cruel and yet beautiful sea. The Blen fired on every enemy vessel and plane and was continually under fire from enemy aircraft during this time.

Ports such as Salerno and Anzio were more familiar than Easington Colliery to Jim. Days and days went by then weeks and weeks without thinking of the pit place he had been brought up in, as he was kept fully occupied with his duties as gunner and quarter master, he had been promoted. Then it was only on birthdays or Christmases that he cast his mind back to far off England. Anyhow memories only cause the anguish of home sickness for his mother, father, sisters and brothers.

At one time Capt. Warren told me how he felt the moral of the ship was very low , he contacted London who told him to let the crew ashore as soon as possible for a short time.

The Blen sailed for Gibraltar where the crew went ashore and no doubt they all sowed a few wild oats. At about this time Capt. Warren left and Captain Peter Dickens took over, he was the great grandson of the famous author Charles.

The next extract is from a book called, The Royal Navy day by Day edited by Lt. Comm. R.E.Shrubb. RN. and Capt. A.B. Sainsbury V.R.D. M.A. Royal Naval Reserve.

10 JULY 1943

OPERATION HUSKY   LANDING IN SICILY.
BLENCATHRA WITH OTHER R.N. SHIPS

9 SEPTEMBER 1943

OPERATION AVALANCHE   LANDING IN SALERNO
BLENCATHRA WITH OTHER R.N.SHIPS

10 MARCH 1944

OPERATION SHINGLE   ANZIO
BLANKNEY, BLENCATHRA, BRECON AND EXMOOR SANK U450

30 MARCH 1944

BLENCATHRA, HAMBLEDON, LOFOREY AND TUMULT SANK U223 OFF SICILY LOFOREY BEING SUNK BY THE U-BOAT

MORE WAS TO COME

Jim said Capt. Dickens was a 'death and glory' man, they continued with skirmish after skirmish, shooting planes down and sinking ships. One day the ship stocked up rather well with fresh fruit and other supplies at Gib. On leaving the rock there was a 'buzz' on the ship. To call a buzz a rumour was like calling spuds potatoes. No ship was without its latest buzz. Sailors like to know where they are going and when and the buzzes kept the Blen crew informed. The latest buzz was that the ship was bound for England - it couldn't be true- it could be - bets were taken if she turned left that they were going home- England home- if she turned right they were heading back to the Med. She turned left with four other destroyers sailing for their beloved England, that they were continually being brainwashed into remembering they were fighting for but thought they would never see again. And would they? The pessimists said there was still a long way to go and Jim who at one time thought he would never see England again was sure now he would, but when? He remembered his mother telling him confidently on one of his few early leaves when he had said don't worry about me she need not as something told her he would sail not always in safe waters but safely home one day. Perhaps the gypsy's prediction comforted her and she consoled herself with believing the gypsy's forecast.

H.M.S. Blencathra sailed into Plymouth on about 1st June 1944 then made for their home port, Sheerness, Chatham. The ship was given a boiler clean and stocked with ammunition and food. For four days they patrolled the English channel. None of the hoped for leave was granted as the invasion of Normandy was pending. The Blencathra was going to take a further part in the making of history. Everyone seemed to know Operation Overlord as it was called was imminent but no one knew when.

The ship was ordered to Milford Haven. As she ploughed her way to her destination the Blen passed a tug towing what looked like a vast and half submerged reel of cotton. Jokes on what this mysterious object could be were bandied aboard - one of them 'a machine for putting a head on beer'. This was actually PLUTO - Pipe Line Under the Ocean - PLUTO.

Two parcels were waiting for their commander, Captain Peter Dickens, the smaller contained details which he handled reverently. They were orders for Operation Neptune, the larger parcel held amendments. Security ordained only the captain could see these documents. As he worked his way through these papers he began to realise the magnitude of the operation. The utter confidence of victory and the amazing detail truly staggered him. The battle experienced Blencathra was to be one of seven thousand yet as he read on it was made perfectly clear what she was required to do and how her part fitted into the jigsaw of the whole complex undertaking. And we know a jigsaw is forever incomplete with one part missing. The Blen noted for her courage and daring, lucky and fast was once again to play her part well.

As Captain Dickens worked with paste, scissors and waste paper basket, calculating his part of the jigsaw and amending the papers the waste paper basket was soon filled. When he was momentarily in the 'heads' his ever soliticitious 'gentlemen's personal gentleman', Able Seaman Gallop who had been trying for hours to get into the captain's cabin to 'clean it up' as he habitually did ditched the contents of the waste paper basket into the fast running sea. Unfortunately as Captain Dickens was away briefly, papers slid from his desk into guess what - the waste paper basket. Imagine the captain looking with horror when he returned to a very tidy cabin - no papers- but the captain, quick to act called Action Stations and the lifeboat crews were soon busily fishing soggy bits of paper out of the water. All was recovered. What did the people of Milford Haven think of this sudden maritime 'Keep Britain Tidy' campaign. I wonder.

If these very important papers had not been recovered would Overlord (the name of the whole operation) have been changed? I wonder.

CHAPTER ELEVEN

H.M.S.Blencathra picked up an enormous convoy of American troopships along the south coast of England and sailed across to France, casting off the night before D-day just as it was growing dark arriving just as light was breaking. The weather was foul and because of this there was no interference from the Germans who were not sure of the date or the exact landing place of Operation Overlord.

The landing beaches which were between CHERBOURG and LE HAVRE were OMAHA, UTAH, GOLD, JUNO and SWORD. UTAH and OMAHA were the American beachheads and the Blen stayed with them to provide cover from enemy aircraft and ships. This lasted all day.

There were nine thousand casualties on these beaches. The noise of battle never ceased, guns of every size firing, aeroplanes flying overhead, men shouting in fear and giving commands. The blue summer sky was black with smoke from the guns. The Blen was under constant enemy attack. Her loyal, skilled, crew now connoisseurs of war, experienced in hunting and killing were now determined to win. Untiringly the guns continuously and relentlessly fired on the enemy, bombarding, clearing the beaches for the allies. The Germans, most of their resources in this area as six divisions of their troops were on training manoeuvres here unluckily for the British, American and Canadian troops , used all their skill to out wit the British. They could not but their unknown and unexpected presence accounted for the high casualty list. What day or month or year it was Jim did not know or care. He cared about trying to defend British and allied troops and most of all fighting so that Britain could remain a free country - never to be Nazi ruled. In the evening, which evening the track of time was lost, the Blen returned to England to pick up, give cover to and escort a tug and barge which was going to lay a pipeline across the channel. That is how the petrol was taken to France for the vehicles and tanks. This is of course was PLUTO - pipe line under the ocean. When the Blen arrived on the French coast with the barge and pipeline she patrolled the beachheads as close to shore as possible. Defending, guarding, attacking, the trusty indefatigable crew, adrenaline flowing continued killing enemy soldiers, sailors and airmen and giving cover to allies and British.

What difference had it made sailing to England? Jim did not have time to think at the time, but later as he went ashore in France fantasised that perhaps he had stepped ashore on to his homeland for was that place called Easington Colliery just a dream ?

As the Blen patrolled the crew watched from their various stations, Jim from his post strapped to his Oerlikon gun and saw old merchant ships being towed into position and then scuttled. Mulberry harbour was being built. These scuttled ships were to form a breakwater so that materials could be landed in calmer waters. The sea was very rough. When Mulberry harbour was completed the Germans who all the time were also on the defensive killing British and allied soldiers, sailors and airmen and sinking ships, started to tow 'human torpedoes' out of Le Havre then cast them adrift on to Mulberry harbour and ships going in or out with troops and supplies. A human torpedo was a machine with a man inside who fired the torpedo at the target and could not miss as he was so close. After he fired the torpedo he hoped the rest of the machine would drift on to the beach as they were not made to return.

In the meantime British Motor Torpedo boats had other ideas, whenever they spotted one, you could just see the glass dome above the water, the M.T.B.s dropped five pound charges of TNT on them and blew them up.

So think, dear reader, of the tremendous noise going on - guns firing at sea and on land and in the air. Every human on the Operation Overlord on the alert and Jim was a cog in the wheel of it. Captain Dickens death and glory man, as were the crew, commander of the Blen thought he would go one better and try to capture a human torpedo. A boat was lowered so that a human torpedo which had been spotted - it looked like a double cigar, twenty feet long could be lifted up with the davits of thU boat. Jim was watching from the rail and volunteered to go over the side. He was tied to a life line, lowered down the side of the ship and he secured the shackle and unscrewed the Perspex dome of the human torpedo- it was like a pilots cockpit. Jim told the German to get out and before the arrogant enemy did so he bent down and touched something in the torpedo. The German said to Jim - one, two, three, boom! They were hauled up by the lifeline together - two enemies and Jim was shouting to the captain "Clear the upper deck". Rolling on to the upper deck Jim ran as everyone else was running away from this deadly weapon. Jim raced the German- forgot he was fastened to the safety line and was stopped short!! He quickly cut the line and freed himself as he was being ricocheted back by the safety line. He was blown into the air by the force of the explosion, fortunately no one was injured. It certainly was not funny at the time but when this incident was recalled at reunions forty years later the crew laughed with Jim about being ricocheted back to danger by a safety line! Just like a keystone cops adventure they reminisced. Also they reflected it had been very fearless and brave and daring of Jim to have volunteered. A veteran John Seldon also recalled with admiration and I listened with pride that he had been the best look out on the Blen being able to spot a seagull on the horizon. John told me how on one occasion Jim had saved the ship. He had seen an aeroplane, a Junkers 88 fire a torpedo at the Blen about 400 yards or more away and immediately reported it - the captain altered course to starboard fifteen and the torpedo ran along the portside about eighteen feet away. As the plane flew past on its course the gunners, including Jim, opened fire and blew it to bits. She turned round to pick survivors up but there were none. This happened in the Med.

Back to Normandy, the human torpedo dented two ships plates and caused quite a bit of damage to the ships side. Later the skipper found out two had already been captured so all that had been in vain.

The naval operation was called Neptune.

CHAPTER TWELVE

When all the troops were ashore and PLUTO was well and truly established and the Germans had been pushed back Jim together with three shipmates went ashore via a liberty boat on to the beach which they had given cover with gunfire a short time before. Bodies were being picked up from sea and sand. What price war, nine thousand men some of them boys, killed on one beach alone, thousands and thousands of lives gone. Will it ever be appreciated? Jim looked at these corpses and hoped peace and victory would be worth all this cost.

They intended visiting the little village near the beach but an ambulance offered them a lift further inland. Jim who by now had no fear for his life accepted, passing fires in the fields and windowless cottages on the way, they ended up in Caen. The French welcomed the British sailors as they walked the streets - a strange sight these young seamen so far inland. The French did not have much to give but plied the sailors with what they had so Jim found himself with an armful of local cheeses presented by people glad and grateful to be rid of the Nazi occupiers. I have tried to find these people since, also the cafe where Jim had coffee but I have not been able to yet but I will keep trying, perhaps when we go to Normandy in June 1999 I might succeed.

Thumbing an ambulance back was an impossibility, they were all full of wounded and dying . An American jeep, its driver a G.I. bemused to see English sailors hitching a lift stopped and Jim and friends hopped in. The jeep was certainly a rough ride. The driver ignored the roads and went across the fields in the tracks of tanks that had flattened the cornfields that Jim had seen burning as he travelled in the opposite direction. Sailing in a rough sea with the waves a mile high, the bows of the ship rising from the sea at right angles then plunging deep into the ocean till the stern was almost vertically upright was one thing when one had the whole ship to slide about in, but this jeep just bounced up and down and Jim who had dreamed of being safely on terra firma wondered if it was so safe after all as being thrown up he was almost thrown out with his French cheeses. He finished up with one on arriving at the beach. When the American asked him how he enjoyed the ride he told him 'I prefer a sail any day'.

On a patrol in the English channel the Blen spotted a U-boat, it was on the surface, on seeing them it immediately submerged. The Blen scraped across the top of the U-boat damaging its bows and astic dome which is beneath the water. The U-boat obviously would be damaged too. The Blen limped to Harbour and pulled alongside the jetty to find out where they were going for repair. Bets were taken for their destination, some for Ipswich, some for Geordie land i.e. the Tyne. They came to the Tyne. Leave for Jim, two or three days at a time. He took two sisters on board, Ann and Hilda and they got plenty of free chocolate and chewing gum and had a good look around the ship. At night the captain brought the cast from the Empire Theatre. Evelyn Laye and her husband and the all star cast.

After being repaired the Blen next went up the Rhine on a courtesy visit picked some soldiers up and took them on a sea patrol. When they came back their officer asked the captain to allow some of the seamen ashore so that they good give them a good time as a thank you. Beer was free. A good time was had by all. Jim spent two days in the sick bay after this outing, he said he couldn't light a cigarette for two days for fear of blowing up. In his hand he had a blood stained crib board when he came to and it wasn't his. That remained a mystery for ever. He kept it as a souvenir and we still have it today.

After this things were quieter, the Blen sailed up the Kiel Canal and arrived in Rotterdam. By way of relaxation the crew, the indefatigable ship's company decided to throw a party for some children who they invited from an orphanage. They built swings and suspended them from the gun barrels, and made a slide from the bridge to the quarter deck. The children had an unforgettable time. By the end of the day all waifs and strays from the docks were on board. By evening when the party was over there was no food left but who cared, a great time had been had by all.

The crew then went ashore and with the locals danced round the statue of Queen Wilhemina. One thing struck Jim amongst all these festivities, the shops were all bare. He enjoyed himself with these good, kind, grateful Dutch people, who welcomed the crew as though they had won the war single handedly. The war was won by the British and allies on D-day you could say. At the end of that night when the crew staggered aboard the officers tried the slide out from the bridge to the quarter deck sliding down in a stage coach like contraption, four at a time. Guns quiet, hostilities at an end but would these young sailors ever sleep routinely and peacefully again?

One of the things that he told was how at sea when sitting on the very small toilet when it was rough if you were thrown forward it was O.K. as you could hang on to the door but when the ship rolled back your back pressed against the plunger which flushed the toilet. He made us laugh the way he told this.

Next they were attached to the Fleet Air Arm as a crash boat picking up pilots who had crashed into the sea off the north of Scotland in the Firth of Forth.

Shortly after this Jim was sent for by the captain to be told he was being demobbed he

PACKED HIS GEAR IN HIS KIT BAG AND WAS HOMEWARD BOUND,

CHAPTER THIRTEEN

1945 the war is over. These young men from all walks of life couldn't believe that life could ever be normal again - that they would live ashore - live in a house- no more gunfire - no more sound of the sea. Jim was given fifty four days paid leave. The ship docked at Sheerness and Jim arrived in Easington one morning - what day of the week was it? Worn and weary? Not likely, he could do without sleep now, he could sleep anywhere including standing up, he learned to do that in that damned war. Had Easington changed? He did not write to tell his parents he was on his way home. He knew they'd be there and phones were something few and far between and very rarely used at this time.

He walked into the yard of 5, Cedar Street, paused momentarily to take the sight of the house in and then quietly opened the back door - the time 7.30 a.m. His dad was kneeling in front of the empty grate, crumpling newspapers in his hands in readiness of lighting the coal fire, a bundle of sticks was on the hearth together with a bucket of roundy coal. On feeling the slight breeze from the open door James turned and there was Jim standing in his naval uniform safely home at last. He ran to his son and embraced him, oh how proud he was of his handsome sailor son and the happiest man on earth now he was home. He ran to the bottom of the stairs shouting

"Mag he's here - he's home".

No need for Margaret to ask who, there was only one she prayed would come safely home. She said later she always knew he would come home unharmed. Something told her - even when he had been reported 'Missing in Action' as he had been she knew he was safe somewhere. She still recalled the gypsy's words 'he will be the first to make you a grandmother' and here he was safe and sound and she wasn't a grandmother yet.

The family was ecstatic to see him. His four sisters, brother Reg and this little boy must be Tom who had been a baby when he went to sea. The talk was about the family, friends and Easington. Fifty to the dozen everyone talking and what had Jim to say he did not want to talk of his exploits - it would seem unbelievable in this ordinary house in an ordinary street in this ordinary pit place. His experiences would sound like the movies one went to see at the Rialto, Hippodrome and Empire. Jim had a most enjoyable leave being made welcome wherever he went but he just wanted to feel ordinary and be as he used to be before the war. But the slamming of a door, the sound of a car backfiring or someone placing a beer glass down on a table was enough to set all his nerves jumping.

One day he was reduced to tears at the sound of his young brother kicking a tin can around the back yard. Would he ever be able to relax? Why must the fire crack, setting one's teeth on edge - he hoped no one noticed how jumpy he was at these everyday noises. If his body relaxed his eyes, his ears and mind could not.

One incident marred his homecoming and almost made him wonder if anyone in Easington cared. Funny how one incident can cut to the quick and hurt. Jim thought he would call at the Tin Club for a drink. He was refused entry because he was not a member! His father was but how could he be? After all he had been through to be barred from going in to a local club where it was known he was now a veteran was unbelievable and unforgivable, because he was not a member! He had intended to apply for membership. When had he had the time? Called up to serve in the forces at eighteen before being old enough to apply for membership and away for five years fighting for ? freedom? James was a fully paid up member and had been for years but that made no difference.

As I write this more than fifty years later I can tell you Jim has never ever had a drink in that club, he was so upset by this slight. He had enough of disagreements and wars and all he wanted was to live in peace and at peace with everyone and to hell with the tin club.

The tin club was closed in the nineteen fifties, the Rialto was turned into a carpet warehouse, the Hippodrome was demolished and houses built on the site. A doctors'

surgery was built on the Empire site after it was pulled down.

Mary N. Bell

MARY

CHAPTER FOURTEEN

My Easington is Easington Colliery. The very first reference I could find to the land that became Easington Colliery is in Whelan's Directory 1894. The extract reads 'The village of Easington which gives name to the ward and deanery is situated on the turnpike road between Stockton and Sunderland, seventeen miles north of the former, and ten south of the latter place. It stands on elevated ground, which gradually slopes to the sea'. The gradual slope towards the sea was to become Easington Colliery.

The map shows a barn, a quarry, a farm and most important the cart track through the fields to the sea which was to become Seaside Lane. A name which conjures up golden sands and blue seas and that is how it was then.

There were many quarries and gravel pits and some farms in the area before the colliery was started. That was all that existed between Easington Village and the sea. It must have been a long journey by horse and cart to take the limestone, sand and gravel to neighbouring areas.

The change was very gradual. There were many pits in the area and they were expensive to establish and to run. Huge profits were made through coal however and in 1899 Easington Coal Company learned there were rich coal seams beneath the North Sea. The site chosen was because the shallow valley seemed a convenient place to establish a pithead. So Easington Colliery was born.

The first sod was cut by Miss Barwick of Thimberly Hall near Bishop Auckland in 1899 and later a street was named after her, one of the first streets of colliery owned houses built around 1909 which were free to the miners together with a regular allowance of coal as long as they worked at Easington pit and their sons were expected to, of course. The houses cost less than £150 to build, they sell at the moment for about an average of £20,000, all modernised. a lot of the houses were built by a builder called Pitt employed by Easington Coal Company whose offices were in Weardale Street Spennymoor.

The coal owners were very powerful and rich and heartless with no thought in their minds but profits. This is an extract taken from minutes of a meeting on 19. 11.1898 less than a year before the first sod was cut to start the work on Easington Colliery. The extract is taken from a book in Redhills, the miners' union headquarters at Durham City.

"Houses. The Owners intimated that it would be necessary in all fatal cases where a colliery house had been occupied by the deceased that such should be vacated before any compensation found to be due could be paid."!!!!

EXAMPLES OF COMPENSATION CLAIMS IN 1899

East Howle. A. Ramshaw claiming in respect of the death of his son, J.T.Ramshaw, a driver, on 19.9.1899. Compensation refused.

Thrislington. Ann Plant claiming in respect of the death of her husband W. Plant, a hewer on August 19th 1899. Award 215 pounds 18 shillings and 1penny.

The Council Offices were opened at Easington Village in 1903 as soon as it was realised there must be a base for undertaking mundane but important work such as sewers, drains, running water, electricity, roads, policing and schools.

There was already a waterworks called Thorpe Pumping Station midway between Easington Colliery and Easington Village. I think it was called Thorpe after the little hamlet which then was a short distance across the fields. After roads were established Thorpe village seemed to be farther away.

Sinkers were hired to sink the shaft. The sinkers with their families lived in wooden huts which were very basic and near the site of the future pit. One of these was years later used as Doctor Irvine's surgery for years. It had two rooms, a front and back door and small windows. They would be heated by wood and cooking would be on open fires, lighting by candles or oil lamps. The toilets would be outdoors, no doubt just a makeshift shed, one serving several families. These huts were situated at the bottom of Seaside Lane as near the work as possible. The engineers' huts were on the cliff tops, a much pleasanter location.

French engineers were the first to try to sink the pit shaft, unfortunately they had to give up because of the 500 feet of limestone rock and water, which covered the rich coal seams. Easington Coal Company would not give up because of the money to made from these rich seams.

They employed the Belgians.

Once again there was trouble sinking the shaft resulting in the death of a man called R. Atkinson of Kelloe being drowned in 1904. A freezing method had been used by Belgian engineers. In 1907 work on the shaft by a new set of experts, German engineers brought to light the frozen body. Robert Atkinson aged 50 years and therefore he must have been very experienced in this work had lived in the sinkers' huts very close to where he was working. He had been born in Kelloe and in the nineteenth century you were known as being of the place where you were born so if you were living in extreme poverty and were in dire straits the place you were living in would send you back to your birthplace to be looked after or claim money from them for keeping you on "the parish", in other words living on charity.

It is time now to give a list of happenings to show how quickly this place grew remembering all the time work was being carried out to draw coal.

<u>In 1904 The Station Hotel</u> was opened known as the Trust for years it is now Devlin's is still be called the Trust by the older generation. Since then has been burned to the ground and houses built on the site.

<u>April 1st.1905</u> A railway line Hartlepool to Seaham was opened. Both of these were ports for exporting coal.

<u>September 17th 1909.</u> The north pit finished freezing and building of colliery houses began on the Southside.

<u>The pit buzzer</u>, an important sound throughout my life, was blown on <u>February 1st 1910.July 8th</u> of that same year the first working seams were reaches. I can feel the excitement all these years later as I type

this. September 14th small cages were put into the North pit shaft. September 15th 1910 the first coal was drawn and at last the first coals for sale left the colliery. . There were already some shops, built as soon as the first sinkers and the foreign engineers came, then Haswell co-operative store opened followed by more shops, butchers, bakers, cobblers, fruiterers, drapers and hardware, (nothing to do with computers) but was nails, hammers, saws, spades, picks and nuts and bolts and anything in that line. An up and coming thriving place.

Lucky councillors who looked after village and colliery wards as so many things were coming here.

At the pit a time clock for the workers was installed in 1911 and cages put into the south pit shaft

In 1912 a Railway Station was opened for passenger service. This was situated under Station Bridge up the hill to the right. A few cottages were built nearby for the station master and porters. (The cottages were demolished and the station closed in the 1970's). The first coal was then shipped from Seaham Harbour.

January 12th 1912 the south pit began to draw coal.

July 1st the railway station opened for passenger service.

July 20th 1912 a Working men's Club was opened - the Black Diamond, the Empire Cinema, and the Miners Hall were opened Sadly as I write the Black Diamond is derelict looking and is boarded up.The Empire has been pulled down and a Doctors'Surgery built on the site. The Miners Hall is still open but in need of repairs which could cost almost a million pounds

In 1913 more colliery houses were built. A contract drawn up specified 33 houses were to be built by Mr. Herbert Pitt of Fox Street, Sunderland, Co. Durham at the cost of £148 per house amended to £150 per house by the sixteenth of May 1913. The drawings and a specification describing the work to be done to be prepared by William Knight of Easington Colliery and by the manager of Easington Colliery and their architects. The Easington Coal Company Limited, 26 John Street, Sunderland in the County of Durham commissioned the work.

The pit had a high accident and death rate. After the death of Mr. Atkinson the next death I found was Thomas Moseby, a coal hewer on 24.7.1912 . It has been extremely difficult to put together a list of men killed at the pit and I find it very sad that a list was not kept anywhere and I have had to find the deaths the best way I could. One death of Mr. Dunn I could not find anywhere, not even at Redhills, the Miner's Union Headquarters despite the fact that the widow received a small amount of compensation for her and the family. I presume this was because she accepted without any question the sum offered. His son told me of his father's death and in Easington Colliery cemetery it is written on his grave killed at Easington Pit.

1913 the Bishop of Jarrow consecrated the Mission church .November 22nd the United Methodist church was opened by Lord and Lady Furness who no doubt were shareholders of Easington Coal Company.

The Hippodrome cinema was opened. There was also travelling shows which pitched marquees and performed plays and circuses visited the up and coming area smelling the money to be spent.

A charabanc service was started by Hirsts from Easington to the town of Sunderland.

March 2nd 1914. The Infant and Junior Girls' school was opened and a separate one for the boys was opened a year later on May 16th. Children from 5 years to 14years were taught here. There were two local Grammar schools, one at Seaham Harbour for the girls and at Ryhope for the boys. An exam for a scholarship was held every year and was called the 11 plus for obvious reasons so the brainier children had the chance of a better education. Places for these schools were competed for at a lot of schools in the area of these schools. The schools were impressive buildings - two, two storey and large with domes (cupolas) and four school yards. The schools had generous sized windows and good sanitary facilities, comprising of flush toilets, across the yards for the children and inside for the staff. There was a shed in each yard for sheltering in out of the rain. Inside - floors doors and window frames were of the highest quality wood. High standards were a feature of many other Easington Colliery buildings then. In fact Seaside Lane, the main shopping street showed a variety of buildings, styles and shapes with a diversity of interesting facades. Several had bay windows and dormers. The Hippodrome, the Miners' hall, Black Diamond, Working men's Club, the two banks, Post Office, the doctor's houses, The Station Hotel are some I recall. Some of the buildings that were situated on the corners had doors on the corner instead of the fronts which added to the grandeur.

In 1914 the North pit changed to bigger cages. I have not yet mentioned accidental deaths at the pit. With difficulty I compiled a list of men killed at the pit. I could find no list so by a lot of research including some visits to Redhills in Durham City (the headquarters of the miner's Union) I hope I have managed to get all the names. To give an idea how difficult it was. The only record I could find anywhere of Mr. Dunn killed in the 1930's was on his gravestone !

May 26th 1915. the Infant and Junior Boys school opened

September 23rd 1915 the Lamp Cabin at the colliery was destroyed by fire, I have found over the years the occasional fire broke out !

1916. The Officials Club known as the Leather Cap was opened. The officials were the only men who wore safety helmets at that time which were obviously made of leather showing I think of class divide between miners and bosses. This was also noted in the allocation of houses the best and biggest reserved for officials.

The first world war was raging at this time and the people of Easington watched a German Zeppelin shot down in flames north of Hartlepool.

In 1917 a German submarine surfaced off Hawthorn Village and shelled an army camp situated there. The North Sea had been known as the German Ocean at one time so they would have plenty of maps of the area. Regardless of war or strikes Easington Colliery continued to flourish.

November 7th 1917. The Wesleyan Methodist chapel opened.

Illness came in the form of an Influenza epidemic in 1918 with a very high death rate - some families lost three or four members.

In 1919 December 18th the R.A.O.B. club was opened at the top of School Street known as the Tin Club, it became known as the Constitutional Club in 1928 and closed March 1994

1920 saw the church hall opened, two ex - army huts built on to the Mission Church and the Primitive Methodists opened a chapel. Wooden huts were built for quickness. Football and Cricket teams were formed. In 1921 an international cap was won by local player Owen Williams playing for Clapham Orient. I could go on but I want you, dear reader, to realise what an up and growing and exciting place this Easington Colliery was at the beginning of the Twentieth Century. The pit people were very versatile, before any buildings were opened they held meetings in each others houses.

Churches and chapels of all denominations were forming youth groups. The Boy Scouts and the Cubs, the Girl Guides and the Brownies, the Sunbeams, the Good Templars and more. There was something for everyone. Every chapel and church had choirs, women's and men's groups who met weekly. A sociable place. Inevitably the pit claimed many lives of all ages. Children under fourteen and women were not allowed to work down the pit. My uncle Robert Duff had started to work down Black Prince Colliery in west Durham at 12 years of age and at 15 he was putting which involved pushing huge tubs of coal, later this was to become the work of ponies. I digress.

Back to Easington Colliery, strikes were called soon after the pit opened, the first being the amount of men crushed together in the primitive cages taking men below ground. The union was one of the first organisations to be formed and every man must become a member and pay his dues regularly or else he was not allowed by the trade union to work. There was a miners' union for pitmen and a mechanic's union for tradesmen. The officials had their own trade union too.

There was a Miner's Welfare Hall also Welfare Grounds which housed tennis courts, football and cricket fields and bowling greens and the "swings" a play area for the children, funded by everyone who worked at the pit, a levy being kept from the pay of all workers and there was something for everyone. Those who did not want to join in could watch or enjoy the pleasant walk around the grounds.

Previous to the cinemas being opened entertainment was brought to the area by travelling actors who performed in marquees. Allotments were planned in different areas, convenient for all, and of course there was fishing from the beach so the pitmen could get fresh air after being cooped up in the foul smelling pit.

Pits were always closing after being worked out and new ones opening and pitmen had to go where the work was. When word got around a work force was needed at this new pit which it was rumoured was going to be a long life pit lasting for more than a century men with their families flocked from all over the country.

New machinery continued to be installed at the pit. The latest always being used to get the coal out of these superabundant seams.

<u>1924 a new road was opened to Horden</u> our next neighbour above and below the ground by Mr. Gosling M.P.

<u>July 11th Peter Lee, a great union leader opened the Aged Miners Homes</u> as the elderly had to be catered for.

<u>1926. The General strike</u> was called and the pit was idle for 30weeks.

<u>1929 The Church of the Ascension</u> was opened by the Bishop of Durham on Ascension Day. Yet another foundation stone was laid for a new church, this time the Baptist Chapel.

<u>November 14th 1929 another fire. The miners Hall.</u> It was reported at an audit that a hundred pounds worth of chocolate was unaccounted for. The excuse soon found - it was reported to have been eaten by mice!!

It was reported that by November <u>1929 over one million tons of coal</u> was produced in one year by 1,491 hewers and putters. Proving that this Easington pit was indeed a first class one.

CHAPTER FIFTEEN

My mother was Frances May Nightingale. She lived at 1,Garden Terrace Sunniside near Tow Law with her older sister Florence together with their widowed mother when she met my father.

My mother was the youngest of ten children, five boys and five girls. Her father, my grandfather was choirmaster and a leading light in the Methodist Chapel. I never heard anyone say that my grandmother went to any place of worship. My mother was brought up in a musical religious family. Some of her brothers could play the violin. Of the sisters my mother was the musical one, she could play the pedal organ taught by her father and the piano and had a very musical contralto voice.

Her oldest brother was about twenty four when she was born and she was in the same class at school as his son. She was always well groomed with hair in ringlets tied back with a large bow and wearing a sparkling white pinafore over her dress as was the fashion. Her brothers son would dawdle on the way to school and arrive his shoes muddied, his general appearance untidy invariably late. Skipping through the leafy lanes doing a bit of bird watching and perhaps climbing a tree to see how many eggs were in a nest. Bluebells and primroses were there in spring, later buttercups, daisies, coltsfoot, ladies fingers, vetch amidst a hundred different grasses - there was no end, every day there was something fresh, something to discover. He passed a pond where tadpoles turned to frogs and new various coloured flies skimmed the surface. In winter it was a fairy tale walk through a wonderland of shapes with the snow heavy on the branches of the trees and bushes and the ground silvery with frost. His journey to school was so interesting. How could a boy pass quickly so many changing scenes? Others could. After being severely chastised by the teacher one day he brought a note from his father the next day. She said "I can sing to that". And the boy quickly retorted "My father can play the fiddle to it". The teacher asked my mother if she was related to this boy as they had the same surname. He quickly replied "Please miss she's me aunt" much to my mothers' embarrassment !!

Her father was asthmatic and died of a heart attack before she met my father. She trained to be a milliner. Florence had had rheumatic fever as a child and was not strong enough to go to work but helped in the house. Another of my mothers' sisters was Margaret Ann, she was trained to be a seamstress. The five brothers were all sent to work at a pit as soon as they were old enough. One of them my uncle Joe was totally unsuited for this type of work. My mother told me how she could go to a shop look in the window and if she fancied a dress tell Joe about it and he would make her one exactly the same without a pattern!!

CHAPTER SIXTEEN

My father, Albert Duff born in the 1880's, was one of eight children. He was the youngest son of five brothers and three sisters. One sister was younger than him. He had a very religious upbringing his parents being salvationists. His parents planned for him to become apprenticed to a stonemason who was a relative when he was fourteen. His brothers started to work down the pit when they were twelve but the law changed the age of boys working down the pit to fourteen by the time he was old enough to leave school.

Just before he was fourteen my father went to the local pit and got himself a job. He then worked at various pits. At weekends he would go to stay with his eldest married brother Tom, who lived at Swalwell who was producing a large family and my grandmother took one of the girls to care for. This seemed to be the practice in those days, a grandparent often took a child from a big family to bring up.

His father was a pit deputy, a very important position at that time, there being very few qualified to hold this position. Two of his sisters never married they were kept at home to look after the house supervised by my grandmother. During the week due to male members of the family coming in at different times meals were served separately.

On Sundays all the family sat down to eat together, that is the male members, my grandmother and Mildred the youngest daughter did. The eldest two girls Isabel and Lizzie served at the table and ate their meal when everyone was finished. Very Victorian and archaic indeed.

My grandfather was injured in an accident at the pit. He was not killed instantly but died a few days later. It was necessary that his body be taken for a post mortem to qualify for compensation from the coal owners. My grandmother declined saying she did not want his body desecrated. She did not get any compensation. She was not destitute as she had two sons living at home keeping her and her two daughters and they all had shares in a coal company called, I believe, Pease and Partners. They eventually lost all this money.

My uncle Bob, the other son at home had a building society account 4802, quite unusual for that time, I discovered a little notebook years later with this information in. Unfortunately it did not name the society.

My grandmother died of a "broken heart" shortly after my grandfathers tragic death. My grandmother came in one Sunday evening after attending the Salvation Army and sat in the chair and died. So that left Bob (Robert), Isabel, Lizzie and Albert still living at 6, Ridley Terrace Tow Law. My father began courting my mother. He was ten years older than her. They met when he was delivering oil to their house, a sideline he had was selling oil, oil lamps, wicks and candles from a horse and cart which were not his but rented. There was no electricity in houses at that time. Oil was used for lighting as well as candles, coal was used for heating and cooking. My grandmother had hoped Albert was interested in the other sister Florence as she was only five years younger than him. But that was not so.

CHAPTER SEVENTEEN

My mother and father married during the first World War. My father rented a house for them to live in but what about my grandmother and aunt Florence? No pensions for them then. After asking if any of the rest of the family were willing to help provide for them, my father who was a kind caring man decided he would take on the responsibility of my mother's mother and her sister. He moved in with them.

A year later they had a daughter and christened her Thomasina after her late grandmother Duff. She was born with a mop of thick auburn hair. She was a very cross child so perhaps it was as well there were three females in the house. My grandmother died in 1924, nine years after her husband.

My father continued working as a pitman. The pits he worked in were drift mines and the pitmen were able to walk in and when time permitted smoke as there were no poisonous gasses. The miners voted for a strike in 1926 and it went on for six months. For Albert this meant six months without pay. May, my mother had begun saving for a new piano as for all they had a pedal organ she fancied owning a piano and learning to play it. She liked to keep up with the times. This was the second time she had saved for a piano, the first money had been swallowed up during a pit strike in 1921. They watched people who had never saved getting free shoes for their children, free groceries and free meals. They wondered if it was worth being thrifty. My father recalled how when he was single a man asked him for the loan of five shillings, quite an amount in the early nineteenth century. The miners were paid fortnightly and the week without pay was called baff week. This man borrowed the money in baff week and paid it back the next week when they were paid, the next weekend he borrowed it again and returned it the following week-end. After this went on for a while he told the man to keep the money and never ask for a loan again as my father said the money seemed to be his no longer as he couldn't spend it as he kept it for the other man to borrow. My father used to tell this tale as a reason for not getting into debt.

When the pit strike was over some pits never reopened. My father felt it was now time for a move. He wanted a more secure looking future. My mother agreed, secretly thinking someday she would return to the pretty village she enjoyed living in. She was a regular attender at the Methodist Chapel, a member of the choir and the local up and coming Labour party together with my father arranging fund raising events she would bake pies and cakes for social evenings. It would be a big step to do as Albert suggested and move to a new place. Florence did not like the idea at all and arrangements were made for her to live with another sister Phyllis at Stowerhouse Farm run by her farmer husband Bob Butters.

A distant cousin of my father's was a boss at Tow Law, he moved to a new deep pit on the coast called Easington Colliery. He visited and told the good workers there was a job and a free house for them if they would come and work there. The snag it was a deep under the land and most important under the sea pit. My father asked about the wages and it was good that was enough for him. Another ticer was it was a long life pit with millions of tons of coal in its depths. Easington Colliery it would be.

My father visited Easington to see the place for himself. He was assured of work and went back to Sunniside to tell my mother all about the place. There was a beach, a novelty for someone who lived in the country, lots of fields, the surrounding country side was pretty, there were denes, plenty of shops and chapels and most important - work. The fly in the ointment father was not due to a colliery free house as he had a daughter and no sons, and as he was now in his forties it was no doubt felt he would have no more children. His oldest brother Tom was already living in a free house as was his brother John. Both had sons John had one and Tom had five sons as well as five daughters. My father was told by the under manager John Charlton he could have a house paid for before he would be on turn for a colliery house. Father had worked at various pits when one closed another opened or else he changed pits to where the most money was to be made. I recall him mentioning Black Prince, Waterhouses, Hedley Hill and Roddymoor so he looked forward to settling to working in one pit for the rest of his life.

My mother's sister and her husband William Nicholson, four sons and two daughters also decided they liked the sound of this new pit and moved too. They were immediately given a colliery house as it was expected that their sons would work at the pit too. Three of them were already pit lads. Four of my uncle Tom's sons worked at the colliery too, the fifth followed when he was old enough.

Uncle Tom and his wife aunt Emily asked my father if he would like to lodge with them. This would enable him to start work at Easington and he could look for a suitable place for my mother and Ena who was a teenager to live in. He could spread the word at the pit and there was sure to be someone who would know of a place eventually. He was an "old" pitman by this time and his advice was often sought by younger men. He said he knew what was what down the pit by the sound of the coal, he said it was always moving and as far as he was concerned the sound of it was like a code and it was just a case of interpreting the code.

CHAPTER EIGHTEEN

My father heard of two rooms being vacant at Easington Village which is situated at the top of Seaside Lane about a mile from the pit. People in the village knowing the workforce at the new colliery needed more accommodation than provided, rented rooms to miners families and also bed and board to single men.

My mother and Ena moved to Easington Village. They brought some furniture with them, among it 2 small chairs called bedroom chairs. These are, to look at, a small dining chair, their once wicker woven seats have been renewed with upholstery. These chairs are very useful for they fit at the dining table into smaller spaces than dining chairs and in fact any time we need an extra chair or two they come down from the bedrooms where they are very useful too. They are so well and strongly made they have so far lasted with regular usage more than a century as I understand they belonged to my grandmother. I digress.

Back to Easington Village, the two rooms were upstairs and overlooked the village green which was flanked on all sides by very old buildings mostly houses. My mother did not think much of this village. There were quite a few grubby looking houses and, she thought, dubious looking characters. There were lots of rag and bone men. One of them had a manually operated roundabout of gaily painted wooden horses which he would set up on the green and charge children for a ride. The horses would go up and down as they went round and round and music played. A carousel was the name of this contraption.

Sometimes traveling players would perform there in the open air. Horses, ponies and goats were allowed to roam freely on the green. My mother had a bird's eye view of this and I think it would be most interesting. Years after this when I had a look through some very old village parish minutes there was a call for a public toilet as to quote " the scenes to be seen at times on the village green were undescribable". The mind boggles.

There were numerous public houses, (I presume they did not have toilets for the drinkers !!), travellers could stay in the Liberality Tavern, now called The Village Inn or the Kings Head or The Half Moon and stall, feed and water their horses before continuing their journey north, south, east or west. Easington Village was a central, stopping 'watering hole'.

There was Leeholme Workhouse in the village too for the very poor and unmarried mothers could have their babies there. To be unmarried and have a child was considered to be a sin in those days, no accommodation or money was provided for them so many whose families rejected them ended up in the workhouses, good job things have changed or we would not have enough places to accommodate all the unmarried mothers of today. They are now called single parents. I can't understand this phrasing as all people have two parents surely.

Tramps could call there for a bed for the night and a meal in exchange for working in the grounds a record was kept of all those who called, some being listed as 'a tramp of about thirty' as though they had no name or perhaps did not want to divulge it. Seaton Holme, a forbidding looking large house that had once been a manse for the Rural Dean of Easington District was home for poor men unable to work and with no one to care for them.

Through the grapevine at the pit, Mr. Gething, a deputy heard my father was looking for a house. He owned a house in Easington Street, no. 5 which became vacant and he offered it to my father and they moved into this house which was stone built, had two bedrooms and two rooms downstairs, no bathroom and an outside flush toilet in a large yard enclosed by a very high wall. No garden which suited my father as he did not like gardening. There was electricity for light. Cooking and heating were by coal. The rent was eleven shillings a week. Mr. Gething began to call for the rent fortnightly when he knew my father would be at work and bring a box of chocolates for my mother. My mother told my father to tell him to call for the rent when he was in and to collect it weekly!!

His elder brother John had a son and daughter and he decided his only son was not going to work down the pit and he moved from his colliery house to a scheme house in George Avenue which was in an estate called Canada also called Holme Hill Estate, still in Easington Colliery within walking distance of the pit. My father decided to do the same. My father began to look for another house with the possibility of buying it. There was a list of houses that Easington Coal Company would advance mortgages for to their workers. Some were called scheme houses, I presume because they were in the coal company's plan for the workers. They were given some addresses; my mother was interested in two. One in Paradise Crescent and the other 10, Tyne Terrace. They asked for the keys to inspect the interiors and were told they could view the Tyne Terrace house but had to take the Paradise one at face value. After looking in the Tyne Terr. house they decided they would take that as they did not know why they could not look in the other one before buying. The fly in the ointment was this house had a huge garden flanking three sides of the house. Father was no gardener. The house he had lived in at Sunniside had a big garden too. C'est le vie he said. Lots of pitmen had allotments and grew vegetables for their families. My father would rather work harder at the pit to make more money to buy them rather than grow his own.

They left Easington Street for the almost new house they were the second occupier in June 1930.

My mother became pregnant with a second child to be years younger than the first About the time my mother was due to have her baby her sister Florence, five years older came to stay to look after her when the new baby was born and to stay as long as she was needed. My aunt's name was Florence Nightingale - a famous name indeed and she was fifty when she got married. I asked her years and years later why she had waited so long in marrying and she said she couldn't bear to change her beautiful name! I digress.

People would say so and so has to be 'into bed' meaning she is pregnant. After the birth was called 'lying in time' and a woman was supposed to stay in bed for ten days after the birth. I'm sure this could only happen if there was a Florrie in the family. Many women had to be on their feet as soon as possible to look after their families.

Later whenever my mother was ill Aunt Florrie came to look after me , my father and mother and she ran the household. She was a valuable member of the family. I thought every one had an aunt Florrie but of course they weren't as lucky as me.

The Tyne Terrace house needed some alterations so my father got a pit mason to do the work. When it was finished the house which had three bedrooms upstairs was downstairs changed from a kitchen, scullery and bathroom to a smart sitting room, perhaps you would call it a lounge fitted with a coal fireplace set in tiles and then a wooden mantelpiece and surround, and a kitchen with a coal fireplace with an oven at one side and boiler for hot water at the other. There was still the bathroom and inside toilet of course.

By 1930 this place was thriving - my mother was a well established member of the Wesleyan Chapel, she was a gifted alto singer and a member of the choir and the sisterhood. The Sisterhood was a Wesleyan Methodist Ladies group who met every Monday afternoon to listen to speakers on various topics and have a short prayer and sing a hymn or two. Thursday nights were choir practice nights. Men went to chapel and had there own bible classes during the week. Trips and concerts were organised and of course rehearsals to be attended. All chapels and churches were busy social places as were the clubs and public houses, the difference being mostly men went as only men were allowed to be members of licensed clubs. Every Sunday there were two grown up religious services, one morning, the other evening and a Sunday school on the afternoon for children. The teachers were the elders of the church. Members of neighbouring chapel choirs came and entertained them and they did likewise. Methodists were teetotal and my parents never found any enjoyment in drinking in pubs or clubs but enjoyed the social evenings organised in the chapel. Chapels were called churches at a later date.

In the twenties and thirties the midwife was a local woman called Mrs. Mather and she delivered many babies at that time earning her qualification by experience and what better teacher. There were two doctors in Easington, Dr. Irvine and Dr. Forsythe. Dr. Forsythe had a nurse always known as the little nurse as she was very tiny and very efficient she was too. She stitched wounds, treated burns, gave injections and gave advice on hygiene. She always wore a long white hat similar to a nun and a sparkling white starched apron. She must have changed it many times during the day to keep up her immaculate appearance. Medicines were dispensed and given out in the surgeries too. Men injured at the pit were taken to Dr. Forsythe's surgery by handcart, this was quicker than horse and cart unless they were already yoked. Later and ambulance was provided. Broken bones and more serious injuries were sent on to the Royal Infirmary Sunderland. The doctor's were important people and both had a very good bedside manner and were on call twenty four hours. Dr. Forsythe was our family doctor. He was extremely well dressed in a tailored three piece suit, sometimes it would be Harris tweed other times navy blue serge and of course a collar and tie and homburg hat. He seemed to know everyone personally, perhaps because he had at sometime visited every home of the patients on his panel (list of patients). A penny a week was kept off every man at the pit for their doctor. The colliery unions donated money to the Royal Infirmary for the treatment of pitmen and their families.

Dr. Irvine was a flamboyant character regularly seen in an immaculate suit with kid gloves, bowler hat and a walking stick. He had a stricter manner than Dr. Forsythe but underneath he had a very kind heart. During the twenties and early thirties he organised free pantomime trips and take the children to The Globe Theatre Stockton. Carriages in a train were booked to take the children and each child given an apple, orange and sweets on the train distributed by himself and Frankie Franks who was a well known comedian who lived in Easington. Frankie's wife, Gene Boyne an actress also belonged Easington. They lived at the village in a house called The Nest and he owned the dog track at the village at that time. Bonfire nights with fireworks and of course a bonfire and Guy Fawkes, Christmas parties with entertainment and always a gift for every child were other pet projects of Dr. Irvines. His surgery was a wooden hut with two rooms that had once been a sinkers hut and was very basic with wooden benches round the sides for seats in one room, the other furnished with a desk and two chairs and was lined with bottles of medicines and he lived next door with his wife and his family. Dr. Forsyth lived on the other side of the road in a large brick house which also housed his surgery

At this time my aunt Phyllis' husband who was a farmer would stable his horses at the Half Moon when he was coming on business to other farms in our area and he would stay at my mothers and fathers home overnight. If it was school holiday time Ena would return with him as apparently she loved the busy life of the farm, the freedom and the horses.

CHAPTER NINETEEN

On the eleventh of October 1930 I was born, at dawn on a beautiful sunny day. The midwife of course was Mrs. Mather. The atmosphere was of happiness. Sixty years later a lady who was fifteen years older than me told me how when she was fifteen she was taken to see this special new baby when I was less than a week old. This was a custom, friends and neighbours as well as relatives called in to see a new baby shortly after birth. I think it was a lovely custom it was as though they came to welcome the newcomer to the world. Another custom was to give a silver coin for luck. Silver coin denominations were from threepence, then sixpence, a shilling- i.e. twelve pennies, a florin i.e. twenty four pennies then the ultimate the huge heavy half a crown which was worth thirty pennies.

Other customs relating to new babies were the mother was not allowed to go into anyone's house - in Methodism till the child was christened (baptised), in C of E and R.C. religion the mother had to be 'churched' before being allowed out before the christening. Being churched meant being cleansed and having your sins forgiven. This practice always made my mother furious and she often compared the compassion of different religions quoting this.

My mother was told she had not to put her hands in cold water for six weeks after the birth. I don't know the reason so of course my aunt Florrie stayed. She would have anyhow. I had a turned up nose which I know to be so by photographs and Mrs. Mather said 'We can't have this' and she advised my mother to stroke my nose downward every day to correct this and this she did and my turned up nose became straight ! The weather was typically of a good autumn, not too cold and the last of the summer sun shining so at a few days old very rare in those days my aunt took me up the village road. There were no houses between the top of our street and the village then, so it was as though walking through fields.

When a child was christened usually two to three weeks after the birth the baby was carried to church by the godmother who also carried a piece of the christening cake which was a rich fruit cake, sometimes with a piece of rice cake, always with a piece of silver all wrapped in a paper serviette and this was given to the first child the party passed on their way of the opposite sex of the child. Each babe had one, two or three godparents. Christenings were carried out on Sunday afternoons during the Sunday school then it was back home for a slap up high tea. High tea being home boiled ham, tongue, and peas pudding followed by fruit tarts, cakes and jelly and custard - all home made. Of course this would depend on each family, but my mother informed me this was the tea at my christening on a very cold day in November 1930. Afterwards those who wished left for the evening service and returned later for a singsong round the organ in the sitting room. My father rocking me and singing to me. We had a wooden rocking chair which came from Sunniside and was kept in the kitchen as it was not grand enough for the sittingroom which held as well as the organ a three piece suite made of a blue and fawn plush material with golden tassels hanging from the arms. The settee was a two seater and one of the arms let down so if you wished to have a nap you would be comfortable. Also there was a dining table and chairs, a leather blue and brown pouffee and a sideboard with a mirror and carved shelves and doors. There were two dumb waiters, which were kept in the cupboard under the stairs until needed, the biggest one which was oblong with two trays when folded acted as a fire screen in the summer. The kitchen also had a table and chairs and a settee, also folding chairs were kept in a cupboard.

Disaster - during the evening of my christening the lights in the house fused - the house was in darkness. Candles which were always on hand were lit so the sing song continued in the dark by firelight and candlelight in the comfortable sitting room, sounds wonderful to me. I had behaved beautifully acting as a contented baby should appearing to smile when awake. It has always been debated whether young babies smile or they seem to do so due to wind. I prefer to think they smile because they are happy.

My non-handy father went to the pit and an electrician returned with him to repair the fault. One shilling and three pence was kept off his pay for as much electricity as he could use together with repairs such as this. The axe, pick and shovel which he used at the pit he had to buy himself were sharpened by the blacksmiths at the pit for one or two pennies an item. He bought the best tools for his work and said Galley's in Seaside Lane was the specialist hardware shop for pit tools of all kinds. This included hammers and other carpenters tools, bricklaying, welding and all other tradesmen and workers needs. Galleys shop was at the bottom of Seaside Lane. Mr. and Mrs. Galley were staunch Wesleyans. Mr. Galley was choirmaster and superintendent of the Sunday school.

The men at the pit had marras i.e. a man they worked with. Also they had cross marras who worked the particular coal yardage they had been allocated by cavils which is something like a draw which they held at regular intervals during the year to see which part of the coal seam they would work. The cross marras worked on the other shifts which meant that each coal face was worked twenty four hours. A good marra was essential and a good cavil was a help. If my father drew a bad cavil which is where the coal was difficult to hew he soon made it into a good one, I presume by hard work. His cross marra was Mick Gallagher. His overman Paddy Gallagher, they said they were not related. My father usually drew the pays which were all the marras earnings for a week. There could be two four or six pays on one note and the money was given out at the pay office at the pit, but it was paid all together so the money had to be divided up, to do this change was needed and every Friday which was pay day. Mrs. Galley who was a cripple would sit at the cash till in their hardware shop and give men change so that they could divide the pay out. She did this service free of charge because they did a good trade from the pitmen. My father also drew the catholic father's pay, sixpence a week was kept from every catholic who was employed at the pit and the pit cashier put the amount on a paynote for the R.C. father as though he was a worker. He handed it over to Paddy Gallagher who in turn handed it on.

Back to christenings. The day after the christening it was the custom to take the baby to three houses. At each of these houses gifts were given to the new baby - e.g. a box of salt- salt of the earth, a bag of sugar to sweeten life and a box of matches to light the way. Sadly this custom died out but it was another of those community customs where visiting kept one in touch. After visiting three houses mother and baby were 'free' to go anywhere.

I was a plump robust baby. My aunts, uncles and cousins frequently visited for holidays and often came for week ends from Sunniside, Tow Law and Roddymoor. My aunt Mary and uncle Will and cousin Edie from Sunniside. Uncle Joe left the pits and bought a newsagents shop at Hebburn-on-Tyne and he and aunt Ethel (his wife) visited often. He bringing his knitting and wearing his fairisle pullover which he knitted without a pattern. We visited them. The only time I saw children barefoot was when I went before the war to my uncle's shop at Hebburn.

Meanwhile I was very close to my mother's older sister Tan, her husband uncle William and their family called Eva, Wilf, Bill, Jim, Mary and Joe. Their surname was Nicholson. Their family seemed to be an extension of ours and I was always extremely happy in their company. I have not mentioned my sister Ena because I can't remember her at this time but I did not miss her because the Nicholson's were my family so perhaps I saw more of them than I did of her. My aunt gave me pocket money from as long as I can remember. It was two pennies a week I can't explain this except to say maybe it was because of the age difference yet all my cousins except Joe were working when I was born. Ena was called Thomasina after grandmother Duff and I was called Mary Nightingale after my maternal grandmother Nightingale. Years later I learned our grandmother Duff was called Tomasin.

Among tales I was told - I was very fond of cheese - still am - and when I was a few months old, sitting on the floor, my uncle Will Carr from Sunniside gave me a chunk of cheese from the table, it was huge as cheese was bought by the pound weight as it was a favourite of both my parents. My mother attempted to take it from me and I screamed and went into a tantrum. This was remembered because I had always been a happy and placid child, perhaps everything had gone the way I wanted before. One day my mam, dad, uncle William and aunt Tan went to Sunderland for the day carrying me to look around the shops. I was again a few months old. We went by bus of course - very few owned cars. As I was pretty heavy Uncle William offered to carry me to relieve my fathers' aching arms. We were in Woolworths store where everything was under a sixpence. When we came to the toy counter my mother bought me a rattle and gave it to me, I promptly hit uncle William in the eye and gave him a black eye.

My mother could not settle for a long time and she frequently visited Sunniside and of course took me. I loved to go. We travelled by bus and had to get the bus from Easington and change at Durham for the bus to

Sunniside. Sometimes we went for the day and sometimes I would be left there for a holiday. I always stayed with my aunt Mary and uncle Will, their daughter Edie was married by then and not living at home. My aunt had a Jack Russell called Peggy. She was extremely house proud. The house was immaculate and she even put socks on the dining table legs so they were not scratched. She had brass fire irons that you could see your face in. The house had two bedrooms and I slept in one and Peggy slept on the bed at my feet. I had never had a bed like this as my mother was known to be very modern and we had highly polished wood bed ends and flock mattresses. The bed ends at my aunts were brass, and sometimes I was afraid I would smother under the feather quilts and sank into the deep feather mattress. It was very comfortable. The covers and sheets were all white and there was a white fancy embroidered valance round the bed. When you lifted the valance to look under the bed there was a chamber pot decorated with flowers.

Downstairs there was a large living room with a black range with an oven on one side and a boiler for hot water on the other. The furniture that I remember was a highly polished table and chairs. A dresser again highly polished which contained tea sets and china that was not in every day use, a stool and a couple of beautiful wooden rocking chairs. On a tall occasional table by the left of the front door which opened directly from the front street was an aspidestra plant in an ornate flower pot. The stairs curved up from the right side of the back door which opened onto a small room (open staircase) in which we ate. Leading from this was a pantry. The largest pantry I have ever seen. You could walk into it. It had shelves all the way round and here was kept the wash tub and poss stick. My mother had a wash house in the yard and our washer was the most modern of the time, it was a tub on legs and a handle was turned round and round which rotated a gadget inside and cleaned the clothes. There was a cold water tap in this pantry as well. So my aunts' house was a novelty to me and guess what more was to come, the toilet was outside. It was kept locked and as there was no back yard it was across a communal courtyard. A brick small building, two steps up and inside another two steps up to sit on a wood bench with a round hole, this was the toilet seat and had a lid. The toilet paper was tissue paper which my aunt cut into squares and threaded with string and hung on the wall. The key was kept on a hook in the pantry with a bottle of disinfectant at the side and when you went to the toilet you carried the key and the bottle. I remember doing this from about five years old. On a morning when my aunt or uncle cleaned the ashes out of the fireplace they emptied them down the toilet. It was known as an ash closet. This ash closet fascinated me. I soon learned how it was emptied. When the ash bin men came they lifted up a square of metal at the back of the toilet on the outside and shoveled the contents into a cart. I watched this regularly from my bedroom window. You have never seen such bluebottles that hovered round this cart, the size of them made my eyes nearly pop. The men always wore a kerchief mask round their mouths and noses.

Every morning my aunt collected the milk from a farm over the road from her behind a pub called as far as I can remember The Rising Sun which I thought was appropriate for a place called Sunniside. The number of men who went in here amazed me. I wondered what they did. My mother would put her nose in the air when I asked and tell me not to ask so many questions, perhaps this is the reason I never found out where the contents of the ash closets went to. Back to the farm. My aunt and I would sit on a wooden settle with a high back similar to that which I have seen at Beamish Museum, and aunt Mary and the farmers' wife would gossip about everyday happenings.

At the bottom of Front Street in which my aunt lived was a newsagent and I would go there for pencils and notebooks to draw and write in. I never kept any of these unfortunately.

With my mother when we visited Sunniside we would visit the farm of my aunt Phyllis and uncle Bob Butters. He was always very busy on the farm. I remember him best sitting in his rocking chair by the parlour fire smoking a pipe talking to me about the animals on the farm. He had cattle, sheep and horses. In the farmyard were hens. His fields were full of corn. It seemed to be an affluent place. In the farmyard were many stables and the cowshed where I watched aunts Phyllis and Florrie milk them squirting the milk into buckets sitting on small three legged stools. The dairy was attached to the farmhouse and was always cool. My aunts showed me how they made butter by churning. Putting the cream in the churn and turning it by hand for what seemed to be hours till it turned into butter. No other butter tasted as good. Aunt Florrie would take me to collect eggs from a henhouse that we had to climb a staircase outside the building to get to. She carried a lined basket to put the eggs in. The toilet was guess where - outside in the farmyard. It was very clean but whereas my aunt Marys' toilet was light and airy this was dark and spooky and I think there might have been spiders lurking in the dark corners.

My aunts and uncle frequently asked me to stay on the farm. I flatly refused. Their sons who worked on the farm with other farmhands would tell me how Ena always stayed all the school holidays at the farm and rode the cart horses bareback. I was always frightened of horses and often wondered if when very small I had been put on a horse and objected. The name Ena didn't mean anything to me. The farm was a friendly enough place. During the day I have also accompanied aunt Florrie to the fields with a huge basket of sandwiches and flasks of tea for the haymakers during harvest I am sure I would have enjoyed myself if I had stayed but the fear of horses was too great. Sadly my uncle was gored by a bull and died. The sons left the farm and my aunts Phyllis and Florrie went to live at Croxdale. My Mother continued to take me to visit them there and I stayed with them for a holiday on my own many times. They had a picturesque cottage and kept a few hens on the edge of a wood nearby.

CHAPTER TWENTY

There were frequent epidemics of infectious diseases. I am four. My head hurts. It is dark. My head hurts and I can feel the darkness. I am lying on the settee in the sittingroom. I can hear the clash of the oven door from the next room and then my aunty puts something warm on my chest and back. It makes me feel comfortable and the blackness goes and there is nothing.

I have been asleep, my throat hurts and my head hurts. My mam stands beside me like and angel. I am hot and my head hurts with a terrible pain. Maybe I can't see, because everything is black or is it always night time. Oh my head, my head -. The oven door slams again and I feel my aunty comforting me with warmth on my body. The head pain is unbearable - then it is gone.

I am in a warm, serene, quiet place. The sky is blue as though painted and the grass is like a bowling green. I am playing with my friend, Doris Sellars - we are sitting on a blue checked blanket. I recognise it, it is the one my mam puts on the lawn on the back garden for me to play on. She says grass is always damp and I must never sit on it without a blanket. Doris has black hair, mine is auburn,we are both plump and four years old.

Doris and I were born in the same month October of the same year. I have known her forever and she is part of my everyday life. She lives in the opposite street Wear Terrace number seventeen and I live in number ten.

We pick daisies and make daisy chains into bracelets, necklaces and hair bands. My mam makes lemon and barley water and sit on the back lawn and drink it. It tastes sour and we screw our eyes up and laugh as we drink it. One day mam gave me some paper and a pencil, and Doris too of course. We drew dolls and birds. Doris can draw everything better than me. My mam says she is gifted. I wish I was gifted like Doris I think her special gift is the one of making me feel happy.

We ate an apple, then planted the pips in our back garden lawn. This was Doris's idea. She is full of good ideas, like this. We sat and watched the ground for a long time. We lost interest because they did not grow. A week later I had forgotten about the pips but Doris reminded me of them. We went to look at the place we had planted them in. We couldn't find it, the grass had grown over the bald patch. Doris said I would wake up and look out of my bedroom window to see an apple tree reaching to the sky, just like Jack and the Beanstalk. She made me giggle and laugh all that day.

Where has she gone? I can't see her or the blanket either. I like this place, it is so peaceful - I wonder if it is Heaven - I have no pain here. Where is Doris?

I do like it here. Shall I look for Doris? I don't know what I should do. My mind feels still. This place is very quiet and there is a motionless I did not feel before. I am alone. I feel a bit uneasy. There is only the sky and the grass. Everything is so still. There seems to be two ways to go. Ahead or backward. Back to where? To the pain in my head? Have I a choice? Something is telling me I have no choice. I cannot understand this something. I am apprehensive. If I had a choice I would go with Doris. I am unsettled. I am not frightened because I know Doris is safe. How do I know Doris is safe? Something tells me. But where is she?

I wish someone would stop saying my name, Mary - Mary - Mary - over and over again. They are making me leave this place and I want to stay here, I don't want to go back to the hurt in my head.

I am back in the sittingroom. It is daylight and my head doesn't hurt now. My mam is saying 'the doctor says she can have anything she fancies - guess what she asked for - chips - she's only eaten one but that's a start. She seems to understand and to hear, thank God'.

Someone gives me some nasty medicine - I refuse it. 'We will get it changed for some nice medicine - here is the new medicine'. They can't fool me by walking into the yard and coming straight back with the same medicine. I will humour them. I have been ill. I laugh and laugh and everybody laughs and the room is filled with happiness.

The next time I go out to play I am going to call for Doris. My mam says Doris has gone to Heaven. I tell my mam I know because I was with her

- why hasn't she come back. Her mam must not have called her name Doris-Doris as my mam had.

When we went to chapel and Heaven was mentioned I wanted to say I had been but my mam told me I must never talk about this to anyone because they would not believe me. I don't know why. If it appeared I was about to speak about this she would squeeze my hand to stop me.

Twenty one years later, after the death of my mother I recalled this event. My aunt Tan and my father told me I had meningitis at the time and my friend Doris Sellars had died from it. The clash of the oven door was kaolin poultices being taken from the oven to be used for relieving the pains in my neck and chest which I complained of and my laboured breathing. My aunt sat with me all during the critical nights of this illness. I had at one time appeared to be unconscious and seemed to be slipping and sleeping 'away'.

My mother never told me I had meningitis as in those days if you did not die from it - it left you deaf or simple minded - . It left me all right - I think ...

CHAPTER TWENTY ONE.

A lot of men kept greyhounds for racing. The greyhound stadium between Easington and Hawthorn was opened by Frankie Franks in 1935, the army drill hall was built, the Rialto picture house was built too and the first film to be shown was The Life of the Bengal Lancers, The first film at The Empire cinema was Al Jolson in The Jazz Singer.

I started school in October 1935. I was five years old. There was no starting at the beginning of a term, you started when you were five. I had never been to Nursery school (there was none) or anywhere to prepare me for school, only my mam and dad saying, Schooldays are the best days of your life.

I was taken to Easington Colliery School and left by my mam in this huge impressive building with the head teacher Miss Craig. Miss Craig was herself, an authorative but kind looking individual. She always dressed in an expensive looking large checked Harris Tweed suit and had her grey hair in the style of Queen Mary, piled on top of her head without a hair out of place. There was no school uniform, so I was dressed in a new dress of a warm material and rubber soled black leather shoes and knee length stockings.

Miss Craig took me to my classroom and introduced me to Miss Foggin and a room full of five year old girls. We did not have mixed schools. Round the classroom walls at five year old eye level the walls were painted green so that we were allowed to chalk on them. All around the ledge under this 'blackboard' were pieces of chalk and blackboard rubbers.

I knew all the Nursery Rhymes as my father recited them to me over and over again, very patiently teaching me. My favourite was

> Two little dickie birds sitting on a wall,
> One called Peter, one called Paul,
> Fly away Peter, fly away Paul,
> Come back Peter, come back Paul.

He would stick a piece of paper on the forefinger nail of each hand and put these two fingers on the chair arm and flick each finger behind his head when he said 'fly away' and lo and behold the finger came back without the paper on. Another flick and the paper was back on each fingernail. It took me sometime to work out it was a different nail he was bringing back. This poem always made me giggle. He also recited poetry he had learned when going to the C. of E. school at Tow Law where he told me his education had to be paid for by his parents. Sixpence a week I think the figure was. I recall I must go down to the sea again, (The Ancient Mariner). It was Christmas day in the workhouse, the snow was raining fast, a barefooted boy with clogs on, stood sitting on the grass. This is from memory of sixty six years ago. Also, The boy stood on the burning deck and another about Mary Ann Cotton who was a murderess of the time. I knew all the fairy tales Cinderella, The Three Bears and The Three Little Pigs and many more. No televisions in those days and very few wirelesses. We had a gramophone and some records. I consider I benefited by my father's patience.

I knew part of the alphabet and numbers as when my father took me for walks we would count steps we took, gates we passed and birds flying in the air. My mother took me with her when she shopped and once a week a man called the order man called from the co-op store to collect an order for groceries and I learnt weights and measures and how to add up this way as well. A huge abacus in the classroom was very useful in adding and taking away. I had a small one at home. A colourful frieze around the top of the room was Aa for apple, Bb for ball, Cc for cat and so on with illustrations. The three R's were the most important lessons.

We started school at 9 a.m. lining up in lines of twos in the school yard according to which class you were in being summoned to do this by the school bell, we were then marched in to our respective classrooms. A teacher was in charge of play ground duties. At about 10.15 a.m. we had ten or fifteen minutes break. Some of us would have milk at this time. I had a third of a pint which cost one half penny in old money. The children who belonged to a big family or were in poor health got free milk. Twelve till one was dinnertime and we all went home, no school dinners. Going home the boys would sometimes play marbles in the gutters at the back of Seaside Lane as they were always kept very clean. Shopkeepers kept the back as spotless as the front. Afternoon school was one till 3.30 for infants and till four for juniors and seniors.

The seniors left school at fourteen unless you went to the Grammar School. Once a week we had music lessons taught us by the headmistress. She played the piano and we sang. Sometimes she would have another teacher play and she would walk along a line of us singing and listen and give us a letter. A for the good singers, B for the mediocre and C for those who couldn't sing a note. I was C. This was no surprise as I had been told by my mother to not accompany her when she was singing as I was tone deaf. We were given lessons in Physical Training, running, jumping and when the weather permitted games in the yard. I wasn't much good at this although I was quite good at country dancing which was also on the curriculum. We had spelling lessons and handwriting lessons. To me the highlight of the week was Friday afternoon and we would gather round the huge coal fire that first winter I started school (this, the first starters, was the only classroom with a coal fire) It had a huge fire guard round it. Miss Foggin would read stories about Milly Molly Mandy and Black Sambo which I suppose would be called racist now. She read Grimm's Fairy Tales and Aesop's Fables. How I loved these stories and wished the afternoon would never end.

At about this time I began to attend Sunday School at the Wesleyan Chapel which was opposite the school in Seaside Lane. It was a one storeyed building very strongly built and at the moment is a new and used furniture, jewellery and bric a brac shop. Back to 1935. Every Sunday more than a hundred children assembled for an hour to learn of the Bible and learn the words and tunes of hymns.

During April every Thursday evening we went to the 'piece practise' to recite a poem we learned for the Sunday School Anniversary and to practise singing special hymns for the event. When I went to the practise my friend Patty Greenwell walked there with me and she continued on her way to the Catholic Church in the colliery which was next to the Trust in Station Road. All children went to their own chapel or church during the week as far as I knew. I frequently asked Pat what she did at her services and she said it was confession. I wondered what she had to confess and asked my mother who just said 'ask her' so I never got satisfaction in asking some questions. Phrases often quoted to me were 'children should be seen and not heard' and 'let your meat stop your mouth' this when I was talking too much at the dining table. I became a good listener. Every day before the main meal of the day my father always said a prayer 'For what we are about to receive may the Lord make us truly thankful' and Thank God for a good dinner' when we finished. I had to say 'Please may I leave the table' afterwards too. I thought this was the case in every family but apparently it was not.

The Anniversary was on the first two Sundays in May. On these Sunday mornings a crowd of children and a few grown ups paraded the streets singing the anniversary hymns and collecting money house to house. An announcer shouted the times of the anniversary services after every hymn. We started out about nine and dashed home for dinner and then get all togged up in best dresses or suits. My dresses were of silk or satin, one I recall was white silk with a frill round the hem which was calf length and a frill around each short puff sleeve. I wore a silver coloured metal hair band, had a bracelet that matched and set off with a string of pearls. Another was green silk buttoned down the front and also frilled, another was of pink and white satin. The first I remember was in the Shirley Temple style pleated from the chest also in pale green another was white organdie with red. and blue dots embroidered on it. Sometimes I wore a hair ribbon bow. If my hair was long my mother would curl it in curlers made of material which she had coiled my hair round the night before and when she took these out the next day I would have ringlets.

If you said your piece on the afternoon of the first Sunday you would say it on the night of the next and vice versa. We sat on the platform with the chapel choir and the congregation part was filled to capacity at each session.

Not many Sundays after this we would have prize giving day and those with good attendances at Sunday school got a book.

During the summer we went to a trip to the seaside. This was called the Sunday school trip. It was for grownups and children. It was always on a Saturday. On the Friday evening we had to go to chapel to collect a sixpenny piece and a piece of ribbon attached to a small gold safety pin. All the next day we had to wear this pinned in a prominent position to show we were with that particular party. - in case we got lost on the crowded beach. We always travelled to these trips by train. The farthest I remember going was South Shields. Places I recall were Seaton Carew and Whitley Bay. Not very far but in those days nobody 'ordinary' had a car so these events were the highlight of the year for some. I was used to travelling as my mother frequently took me to the place she had 'emigrated' from so I thought I was a seasoned traveller.

Every child was with a grownup- parent, aunt, cousin or older brother or sister. We always took something to eat with us. Some would have meat pies and pasties specially baked the day before, others sandwiches. Home made cakes were on the menu too. Wooden huts were on the beach and sold pots of tea or jugs of hot water for anyone who took their own teapot. Wicker shopping baskets were fashionable and were just the right shape for carrying picnics. Shoes filled with sand, coming home we would talk of how we had spent the sixpence, how we had plodged in the sea and maybe someone had fallen in fully clothed and cause a laugh. We compared sticks of candy rock which had the name of the place right through and we debated how it was done.

In 1942 the Wesleyan chapel united with the St. John's Methodists because they had a good building the Wesleyan one being condemned as I have already written it is still in use today. I do believe attendances were dropping in the churches then.

CHAPTER TWENTY TWO

Shipwreck in 1936. Loaded with a cargo of timber the West Hika on January 15th was making for the shelter of Seaham Harbour. The weather was very bad, the sea rough, visibility zero - she ended up on the rocks at Beacon Point. She was there a long time and most of Easington went to stand on the cliff tops to look down on her decks, so close inshore was she that this was possible. Some went on to the beach but more could be seen from the vantage of the cliff tops. I remember being taken to see this by my cousin Eva Handy nee Nicholson together with her husband Bill and their daughter Margaret who was the same age as me, five years old at that time. We were well wrapped up for the day which was pleasant though very cold. The ship looked to be on the sand to me with a little shallow water rippling round her. I remember how clear the water looked. I do not remember seeing any of the crew. Many attempts were made to refloat her. A tugboat tried to pull her free but this ended when one them broke and the tug smashed into the rocks. The cargo was thrown overboard in the hope that a high tide would lift the ship free but this also failed. A reward was later offered for any timber washed ashore but much of it ended up as allotment fences or pigeon lofts. The chance of free timber was too much for the local men. Salvage men dismantled the wrecked tugboat while trying to make a road out to sea for the West Hika. Only the boiler of the tug remained and is there to this day, I am told. It could be seen for years at low water. The ship was finally released by men blasting away the rocks which held her and a much larger tugboat especially hired for the job pulled her into deeper water. She was towed away to be broken up for scrap - an ignoble end to fine ship.

Taffy Williams was hired as night watchman to guard the ship. He was a local character who was a bare fist boxer and was one of the best. He still lives in Easington (died since I wrote this) and his daughter is one of the receptionists at the local doctor's surgery. She is now retired.

CHAPTER TWENTY THREE

Tyne Terrace where I lived and Wear Terrace opposite consisted of thirty houses. The children were a tight little community. At the front of Tyne Terrace was a sand quarry and it was a sheer drop from the path down the front of the top of the street, further down where I lived was a field where poppies grew and other wild flowers and horses grazed. Along the top of the street ran the beginning of Holme Hill Lane. On the left side of this lane at the top of Wordsworth Road was a small quarry which is now filled in and houses built on it. Just as the lane veered to the right there were two gateways - the left one led to a farm, the right one to another quarry. We children from Tyne and Wear Terraces played on the edge of this quarry. The edge was about ten feet wide and this quarry was no more than six feet deep. We thought of this as the 'proper' quarry as it had hoppers in. Running alongside the grassy edge where we played games was a man made oblong shaped concrete pool of deep blue water. I never found out why this water was blue or what it was used for but I imagined it was like the Mediterranean Sea.

My brother in law (Joe) was a builder - my sister got married I don't remember anything about this, she must have married around 1933. They had a baby who I do not remember as a baby but as a toddler. Her name is Joan. Joe's lorries frequently came into the quarry and one day he let me sit under the hopper while it was being loaded with gravel. The noise was terrific and I was rocked about in the cabin, as the lorry left the quarry water poured from the sides. Lorries came in and out constantly.

Sometimes we children planned to go on picnics. Early on a morning we would set off with canvas bags like a satchel slung over our shoulders. Inside the bag would be a bottle of water, and sandwiches. Mine were usually lettuce, others had jam or paste and we would swap. We travelled the full length of Holme Hill Lane and came to Canada walking up the side of this housing estate we were soon at the entrance to Petwell Lane. By this time we would have drunk our water. Half way along there was the old maids' cottage. We went past this house very quietly and quickly in case we were seen and they might 'catch' us/ We never did anything wrong to be caught for so I don't know why we were frightened, we maybe thought they were witches. Just beyond the cottage was a spring we would fill our water bottles here with the cool crystal clear water. At the end of the Petwell Lane we turned towards Hawthorn, at the bottom of Eagle Hall bank we turned to the right and we were at our destination, the Mill Race. There was a quicker way than this across fields to the Mill Race but this was the more exciting way. There was a stream there with a bridge across. We plodged here and across the little wood bridge was a glade of trees. If you walked with the flow of the stream you came to the beach.

In this place, the grassy field, the shade of the trees and the shallow stream we spent most of the day. We swapped sandwiches. I can tell you that the nicest meal you can eat on a hot day after a long walk is a lettuce sandwich followed by a jam sandwich washed down by spring water drunk straight from the bottle, feet dangling down the side of the stream in the babbling, running water.

We were a mixture of children, ages four to fourteen, both sexes. When someone thought it was time to go home we set off to walk alongside the stream. Towards the end of the stream which was through Hawthorn Dene. Almost under the viaduct were two small cottages. We could have bought a soft drink here and sweets but we did not have any money. We climbed up a small hill and walked along the railway line - we could have continued and found ourselves in the pit yard but we would have had to walk up Seaside Lane. After a discussion we usually opted for a different route through fields up Beacon Hill, past two farms into Canada. In one of the fields there was a spring and we would have another refreshing drink here and continue on our last leg of the journey home.

Having reached Canada we walked along Holme Hill Lane and were soon home. Tired, happy and hungry and ready for the 'high' tea waiting for us. We were never in fear of our safety nor were our parents. Happy, happy thirties.

Another day we would all go to the cliffs as Arthur Jordison, Clifford Sumner and Raymond Wilson were camping out. These were the older boys who did not accompany us on our walks and did not join in any of our games because they were working or thought they were too old. Nevertheless we decided to visit them. We had very hot summers but occasionally we would get caught out in a thunder and lightening storm, this day the weather was idyllic. When we got to the cliffs the heavens opened and we all piled into the tent. We were warned not to touch the sides as it would rain in if we did. The temptation was great. I often wonder if it did rain in.

Names from those days are Dorothy Adamson, Jean and Olga Martindale, Jenny Ramage and her cousin Maurice Jackson who lived with them because his parents had died. Jean and Derek Blackburn, Douglas Hind, Jack, Alan and Mary McCartney, Elsie, Bobby and Jack Mawhinney, Jean Curry, Noble Metcalfe, three Wilkinson girls, Pat Greenwell, the Dodds, the Carrs and the Mills. There was a crowd of us.

A year or so after this the younger ones of us (the youngest would be eight) decided we wanted to camp out. After much persuasion our respective parents agreed we could camp out at the top of the street. It was a very uncomfortable night, we did not have camp beds but slept wrapped in a blanket and found out the field was very stony. This made me recall the story of the princess and the pea. How she knew she was a princess because when a pea was put under the bed mattress she felt it. I was just me and that night all of us were cured of our yearning to camp.

The pit was on short time before the second world war and at a certain time my dad would say stand in the yard and listen for the buzzer. If it blew the men were laid idle for that shift. Sometimes dad would come home and say the pit is 'lowsed out' this would mean there had been a fatal accident at the pit. I often heard my dad say 'Another sixpence or shilling of the note this week'. My mam did not seem pleased at all about this and it was quite a while before I realised it was because that meant someone else had been killed at the pit and she was very upset for obvious reasons.

My dad would take me for walks and would stop and talk to other pitmen. I heard them talk of men 'barred in'. I soon learned this meant men trapped by falls of stone. Some falls were according to the talk too trivial to be reported. One that was serious had happened in 1929 shortly after my father started work at this dangerous pit. Three men were barred in for several days before they were dug out and rescued. Often my father and his friends would sit on their hunkers when standing at a corner end as they had to down the pit because of the low seams. Sitting on their hunkers they were the same height as me, when I tried it I fell over. This method of sitting was bending your knees and sitting on your heels!

I didn't mind when the buzzer blew although my parents hated it. To me this meant my dad could tell me stories of his father who I would never know. One of them was his father called him to the front upstairs window to watch a boy chasing ducks in a nearby allotment. "See that boy" he said " He thinks no one can see him but we can. Remember if you do anything wrong someone always sees you even if you do not see them." I wish I had known my grandfather.

My hair grew despite the fact that I had been born bald. My mother thought I was going to be like my father, have very thin hair but my hair grew to be very thick and auburn. My father would wash my hair once a week and as hair dryers had not been invented then he dried my hair with a towel and I would kneel between his knees as he patiently dried it and he would recite poetry to me and tell me how he and my mother met and stories of how he was shorter than his six foot tall brothers because his sisters allowed him to smoke his father's pipe when he was nine years old and many others. I wonder if men of today spend as much time with their children. His favourite song was "I met my thrill on blueberry hill" and he sang this to my mother when ever he heard it on the wireless and she would smile at him.

CHAPTER TWENTY FOUR

1937 the pit head baths were opened, we had a bathroom fortunately. Most people did not and the pitmen bathed in small tin baths and sat on a stool (cracket) and bathed that way, usually in front of the kitchen fire. My father used the baths, it saved bringing his pit clothes home very day. Sherburn Hill Store in Seaside Lane burned down and most important Easington Secondary Modern School was opened on September 1st 1938, so children over eleven were transferred from the Junior school to this school relieving the overcrowding.

On Coronation day in 1937 all children were presented with a tin pencil case.

I heard my mam and dad talk about the Great War - the last war, the war to end all wars - four long years they said, 1914 - 1918. They were civilians, whatever civilians were. Food was scarce, it had to be queued for - black bread - no treacle - no sweets. Fortunately they had lived in a country place so there was a limited amount of dairy produce and fresh vegetables but in this pit place at the coast the fish out of the dirty black sea would not be worth eating if there was another war. My dad had a medical during that war and he was grade two, so he was never called up to serve king and country, two of his brothers were. They were grade one. Guns were fired, men killed, zeppelins came over flying in the air - shores were bombarded in the last war - and we lived on the coast.

I was a frequent visitor to Mrs. Lizzie Hinds house, she lived at 7, Wear Terrace just across the back street. All of us kids were always welcome. Years later I realised Lizzie loved a bit of gossip and us kids, we were proper little chatterboxes.

The topic this Sunday morning 3rd September 1939 was that war was imminent. I told Mrs. Hind that my dad was a civilian in the Great War because when he was called for a medical he was grade two. Lizzie sniffed at this and said "Well he never loses a shift at the pit". Do you think he'll go away in the army if we have another war I asked. " No he'll work every hour God sends down the pit" was her reply. Lizzie's husband was noted for being work shy. Unfairly because he was very musical and preferred to play in a dance band to working at the pit so lost many many shifts.

It was a lovely sunny morning, the cloudless sky was very bright blue and the grass in the back garden a rich emerald green. Douglas Hind and I were playing 'catchy' with a bat and ball on their back lawn. The buzzer from the pit blew - wailing through the still warm September air - we stood still as if we were playing statues. Everything seemed to stand still even the midgies stopped in mid air.

Mrs. Hind hurried out of the house, "You'd better go home Mary the war has started". War had been declared, I rushed home across the back street. Questions rushing through my mind - would we have food - would I hear the guns - would my dad be called up for the army. My dad was too old to be called up in this war - my dad had always been old, probably he was grade two in the last war because he was too old and then I remembered his two brothers who had served in the army during that war were older than him!

I remembered a new word I heard at the time it was munitions - I think it means something to do with bombs. Would the Germans bomb the pit.- they knew where it was, they had sunk it in nineteen hundred and something my dad told me. It was Sunday - would I be able to go to Sunday school today now that war has started and we are at war - they might bomb the pit today. Thoughts tumbled through my head.

I reached the gate and went in to what had been my lovely safe home - was it safe now What about the bombs? I looked forward to my Sunday dinner , we always had a great big roast of meat or leg of lamb - usually beef - or it could be a leg of pork today as there is an 'r' in the month - but we couldn't have this today - war has been declared.

I ran into the house, there is my beautiful mam I love so much, she hasn't changed for all we are at war today, yesterday we weren't at war - today we are. "Dinner won't be long Mary". I looked and everything was as normal just as though it was any Sunday. The beef was there, the yorkshire pudding and every vegetable under the sun - I hate vegetables- I have a lovely skin because vegetables are good for your skin, my mam says. She makes me eat them and I hate vegetables. I hoped there would be no vegetables during the war but here they are on my plate.

Funny nothing changed when they said 'War is declared' - we even had cream cakes for tea. Mam had said you don't have jelly and custard and cream cakes during the war, but we had it for tea that day.

I didn't think wars changed life. Everything was just the same that day, I even went to Sunday school. Nothing happened today - the sky was as blue - the grass was as green. I was disappointed.

Olga Martindale a special friend of mine moved. The Carr's, Jean Curry, The Sellar's, Jenny Ramage and Dorothy Adamson and when I next went to school and Sunday school familiar faces were missing. Their fathers I was told had been sent to factories to work and taken their families with them. I didn't know they were going till they were not there! I never saw them again. The pitmen were not exempt from war service at this time.

CHAPTER TWENTY FIVE

My mam was very musical. She played the piano and organ and had a very nice singing contralto voice. She came from a musical family. With a surname like Nightingale it seemed natural to me. We often had people coming to our house to practise singing for a concert or cantata or suchlike to be performed at chapel. The Messiah by Handel is a favourite and Mrs Bellis, soprano, Mr. Joe Caygill, tenor and a bass singer and of course my mother and before they moved Mr. and Mrs. Bond would come and rehearse their singing for the quartet. Every day my mother played the piano and sang. Her brothers played the violin and her sisters were all good singers. I never heard my uncles play the violin. Her father was choirmaster at chapel at Sunniside. Unfortunately he was dead before I was born.

My dad had a lovely low singing voice. He sang things like, " Zacchias was a very little man", "I'm H.A.P.P.Y." and "My cup's full and running over" to me with all the actions. To my mam he sings Hoagey Carmicchael's "I found my thrill on crawberry hill". Music is for enjoyment I knew this because everyone who came to our house enjoyed the music so much.

My mam sent me for music lessons. Dad said, you can always try. I enjoy playing the piano and singing, but when I sing my mam stands very still like a statue, holds her breath, half closes her eyes and then says 'That's enough". She then breathes again and says "You don't take after me". Well if I take after my dad I should be musical because I think he sings beautifully. He loves listening to my mam sing. When she has friends in he listens to them but never joins in. My mam never allows me to join in either. So when friends and relations start to sing I get a book out - reading or writing. They think I am such a quiet little girl.

Sometimes it is time for me to go to bed before the musical evenings are over. I don't mind because I make stories up about a fairy in a gooseberry bush. I continue it night after night, just like a serial. My mam says I was found under a gooseberry bush. Another story I made up after seeing the lion who comes on at the beginning of the M.G.M. films. One story I grow bigger than it after changing into a lion and chase it back to Africa, far, far across the sea. Another story I shrink it to mouse size and send a cat after it.

After a few months my music teacher Mr. Phillips had to go away to the war. My mam arranged for someone else to teach me and then decided it was a waste of time me going for music lessons. My dad gave her the look of I told you so. My mam said "It's a pity she takes after you". I can't understand this as my dad has a lovely deep soothing voice when he sings to me. My mam says he sings out of tune. I sometimes play the piano and sing. I play the medley with my right hand and vamp with my left. Vamping means I hit a chord (any chord) at the lowest end of the keys and then one half way up, just below middle C in rhythm with the song I am singing. Oh yes I sing at the same time I play. My mam shuts the sitting room door, then I hear her shut the kitchen door. Eventually she comes back to the sittingroom and says "Mary, try to listen to yourself as you sing and play" I tell her I am and don't I sound good. She says "no, it is terrible - can you not hear all the wrong notes you are playing and singing - you are out of tune", She continues with "You sing just like your father". I think this is alright because he sings so well. My mam says this is not so. We are both tone deaf and if I must sing and play please wait until there is no one in the house. That is never because I am never left alone.

It is funny (peculiar) because about this time at school Miss Craig the headmistress took our class for a singing lesson. She divided us into A- good singers, B - can sing and C can't sing for toffee. She said I was C and I had to sit down as the class were practising for something. I don't know what. I can't understand why Miss Craig said I was C because I sang very loudly and clearly when she listened to me. When the class practised I imagined I was a famous soloist, singing with the school choir in the background. When I told my mam I did not sing at school she said she wasn't surprised.

My cousin Joe is a lovely singer. He comes to our house, my mam plays the piano and he can sing anything. When he finished a song she actually clapped one day. Apparently he has an ear for music. I think I sound like him but my mam says I do not. She explains patiently that I must listen to myself singing with the other people and I should hear the difference in the notes I sing. It sounds the same to me. If I sit next to her in our chapel, which is not very often as she is in the choir, or any other chapel she says I must not sing as I put her 'off'. When my mam goes to chapel on a Sunday evening, if it is a fine night my dad takes me for a walk. We stop at a little shop and get some sweets, pontefract cakes, marzipan cakes or cherry lips. My favourites are Silver Link toffees, they are covered in milk chocolate. My mam often says she does not know where I get my 'common' tastes from. She likes the best chocolate or chocolates only. She looks at my dad as she says this. I take after my dad for not being able to sing and I have his common taste in sweets. I am glad I don't take after him for hair, he is nearly bald. I never tell mam about dad buying sweets for me on a Sunday as she says it is a sin to spend money on a Sunday. I am not allowed to knit or sew on a Sunday either. I read The News of The World and do the crossword. I am a dab hand at it. The trouble is the clues have so many double meanings I don't know how anybody gets it right.

My mothers brothers and sisters from around Sunniside visit us. They like the sea air. My cousins visit too. Some of them live in Easington. I love them to come to our house. I wish I had a hundred cousins. My mam says I have.

My cousin Mary has lovely dancing brown eyes. Her hair is shining black and she is always well dressed. She is very pretty and comes to visit us and brings her boyfriend. I want to be just like her when I grow up. She can sing too. Her boyfriend is called Chris Preston. He has the loveliest wavy hair I have ever seen. He is musical, sings beautifully, plays the piano and the mandolin. We have some great evenings when they come. Mary talks to me when Chris is teaching mam to play the mandolin. She is always smiling and I can feel happiness coming from her, Chris has the same happiness about him.

Sometimes when Chris and Mary are singing with my mother I am dying to join in, but I know better. Sometimes Mary just sits and listens with me. All the people who come to our house, we have the preacher from chapel on a Sunday sometimes for dinner and tea and we have prayer meetings during the week seem to think I am quiet. I am not. I make words up to the music. Different words to those that they sing and I enjoy myself making stories up about all the people.

Chris and Mary come one day and Chris is in army uniform. He is a soldier. Chris is leaving his mandolin for my mam to learn while he is away for the duration of the war - I don't know how long that is. I am not very good at measuring time. Mary is rather quiet on this visit but Chris is not, he laughs and sings as beautifully as ever. I want to tell Mary I will always be there even if Chris is away, but I can't find the words to say. When they go away my mam says we must pray for Chris every night, mentioning him by name.

It is round about this time corned beef appears at home. My dad makes a great joke about it. We have it with fresh tomatoes as a rule. When we had no bacon or meat ration left we had it with new potatoes with butter on one day. My dad says the spring cabbage we had with this meal was the best thing about the meal. I hate spring cabbage so I think the new potatoes were the best. I don't like corned beef very much. One day I was coming home from school and one of Jimmy Wilson's (father of Raymond) big cart horses had its foreleg down a sink in the side of the road. Some men were trying to get it out. I did not stop to watch but ran home to tell my dad. He said 'Oh they'll have to shoot it, we will have corned beef tomorrow'. He reckoned corned beef was dead horse. We did have corned beef the next day - so I wonder?-----

Coming in from school one day my mam was very sad. She said Chris was missing in action, we might never see him again. Not even when the war is over. She said I must be extra specially nice to my cousin Mary. I wanted to see her so mam said, "Go on then but be careful what you say". I went to my aunty's house to see Mary. She looked very sad but she talked to me. I noticed she didn't smile when she talked as she used to. But she is as nice as ever. I think she is prettier even though her eyes don't sparkle now. My mam is always talking about Chris. She says it is not right that she has his mandolin. My dad says that Chris would wish her to be learning to play it wherever he is in this world or the next. mam says , yes but she thinks his relatives might feel better having the mandolin as he held it and played it and it might be a comfort to them, so she sent it to them.

My mam did not sing or play the piano for a while at this time. I came in from school one day and I felt there was something good in the air. My mam said Chris is safe, he had been captured by the Germans. My dad had a funny look about him as though she had used the wrong word in saying 'safe'. He did not contradict her in words, but his silence seemed to. My mam says she hopes Chris is getting enough to eat and the guards are kind to him, My dad still did not say anything. She asked dad what happened to prisoners in the First World War and my dad ignored this question as though he had never heard. 'You shouldn't have sent the mandolin back. Chris will think you will be playing it like a connoisseur when he comes home'. My mam is the quiet one now. Dad and I are sitting on the settee, he puts his arm around me and starts to sing in his quiet low voice - The Old Rugged Cross - and I join in the chorus. Mam closes her eyes but she hasn't got the 'shut up and don't sing expression' on her face. She looks calm and serenely sad. When we finished the hymn, mam opened her eyes, came across the room and kissed dad on his bald head.

When I go to my aunty's next she says I must not mention Chris unless Mary does. I go on a Wednesday afternoon when there is no school and the shop she works in is closed. Her laughing brown eyes have not got their laugh back, she says has my mam told me about Chris and isn't it good news? I say yes but I wonder to myself if it is good news or not, will we ever see him again.

After the visit I walked across the field towards home and I thought what it must be like to be Chris locked up in a prison. I stood on a hillock and looked towards the sea. Chris was across there somewhere. He was in Germany in Stalag something or other. After the war we learned he was in Poland. Standing in the field I could see nearly all of Easington, the pit, the houses and people walking about - all free. A dog was running round in circles and a horse was grazing in a corner and I was standing there. We were all free. What is Chris thinking about at this minute in that prisoner of war camp - ?

When I got home I was crying and my mam said I hope you didn't cry in front of Mary. I told her I didn't. When I went to bed that night I made a story up of how I helped Chris to escape and come home.

The next day my dad said he was getting an extra ration of a couple of ounces of cheese because he worked down the pit. He offered to swop my meat ration for his cheese ration. I said he could have my bacon ration too. I love cheese but I don't like this war very much

CHAPTER TWENTY SIX

Before the war started April 26th 1939 the British Legion Club was opened. The Royal Berkshire Regiment was billeted in the church hall, there was a regiment billeted in the Welfare Hall and later they took over the houses in East side Station Road that had cellar kitchens. They were laying barbed wire along the cliffs and we were forbidden on the beach. They also built concrete lookout posts which could be called a bunker. We were preparing for war and it brought home to the population how vulnerable we were. In Hawthorn dene there was supposed to be a big gun called Big Bertha and I had every reason to believe this because during air raids I could see from my bedroom window as I paused to look out before going for shelter, bullets flying through the air.

At the beginning of the war I heard of people being called up, going into munitions and helping the war effort. I asked my dad if he was going to join the Home Guard, he answered puh, I know that means no or not likely. My mam talked of going into munitions and I wondered what I could do.

Everybody was issued with a gas mask in a cardboard box. My mam bought me a leather case to put mine in as she said the cardboard was common and would soon drop to bits. Everybody was given an identity card with a number on it and we were advised to keep this number with you at all times as if you were killed or wounded in an air raid it would be easier to identify you. Which was pretty scary. I wore an identity bracelet with my name and address on it. I memorised my number and I will never forget it, FHIV 22.3.

Every day in the school hall we were asked if we had a hankie, I always had two, one to use and the second one I kept in my knickers pocket so I always had one to show in the hall. I sometimes lost my first hankie, that is why my mam always put a handkerchief in my knickers pocket. There were no paper hankies at this time. I found the gas mask case was useful to keep my hankie in together with my 2 and a halfpennies milk money. For a halfpenny a day I got a third of a pint of milk per day. I was not always keen on this but my dad said 'Feed them when they are young and they can weather life's illnesses as they grow older'.

Air raid shelters were built near the school. Until they were finished I only went to school 3 half days a week - I liked school but I liked the days off better because my dad who at this time was always in 10 o'clock shift, which meant he started work at 10 p.m. and arrived home at about 6 a.m., always seemed to be around and he would tell me how England's foundation was coal. How we were important, England was built on coal and needed coal for lighting, heating, and making such a variety of things. The steel, iron and glass industries depended on coal. He told me that in the last (nineteenth) century women and children were employed down the pit. His brothers had started work when they were twelve but by the time it came to his turn to work the law stated that no women or girls could work down the pit and boys had to be fourteen years and on his birth certificate it stated the date he could start work. His parents wanted him to be apprenticed to a stone mason but he wanted to be a pitman and he went to the local pit and got himself a job, he was a datal boy, then a putter, a hewer and then a stoneman, better paid jobs as he got older. He told me how important families owned the pits, some were good employers and some were not so there was often the problem of safety and frequently there were strikes but he stressed that striking was no way to settle disputes the best way was to talk no matter how long it took because the coalowners could survive for ever without British coal as it could be imported from poorer countries. Miners could not survive long by striking and in his experience no good ever came of a pit strike as the pitmen always went back to work worse off. He told me of the ponies employed down the pit. I was astonished to hear there were no toilet facilities! There had been many pit disasters and gas was a problem and he explained how the air was circulated round the pit. Pit ponies were accidentally killed. Roof safety was another problem and wooden pillars called props were used to shore the roofs up as the men hewed with their picks. Coal was going to be very important in this war.

Some of the older and bigger girls, the school now was for girls from five to eleven, so at nine, ten and eleven year olds were 'big' to me, were chosen to be shelter monitors. My ambition was - to become a shelter monitor. That's what I could do to help the war effort. Unfortunately I wasn't old enough. My mam had taught me to knit, sew and embroider as she was always busy with some craft or other. Everything in our house was embroidered, the pillowcases, cushion covers, chair back covers, tablecloths even handkerchiefs. The net curtains, doilies and table centres she crocheted. She was always busy and as she did these things she would give me a small ball of wool to knit with or cloth to embroider. This stood me in good stead towards the war effort as our head teacher now I was upstairs in the juniors and no longer an infant, Miss Wardell together with the W.V.S. ran a War Comforts Fund. They sent warm hand knitted scarves, gloves, mittens, helmets and socks to members of the forces who belonged to Easington. She got the addresses by calling names out of anyone serving in the forces and if you lived near you were asked to call at that address and bring it back to the school. She organised the parcels to be sent and always included a ten shilling note in each parcel as it was well known the armed forces were defending us but were paid a pittance as all money was going for munitions. Every class every afternoon had to knit and at first you were given cheap, hairy, khaki, navy or air force blue to knit with. When you proved you were a good knitter you were then allowed the better smoother wool. I only knit one hairy, khaki scarf and then I was on to the better wool. By the time I was ten I could knit the more complicated helmets and turn the heels of socks and knit gloves with no effort. War savings was another way money was collected for the war effort, I took money to school for war stamps and my mother also bought some every week from someone who sold them door to door. One thing that irked her a bit was she had to pay a tax which everyone who owned their house (or had a mortgage) had to do. This was to help to pay for war damage to any houses. This was as well as paying council rates and water rates. I knit, for my war effort.

One term I was milk monitor and with another girl had to carry crates of milk for our class into the classroom and when every girl had drunk their milk carry the crates back out again. The teacher always gave the straws out, I fancied that job.

One term I was the ink monitor and I filled inkwells in the playtime, I liked this as I got blue finger ends and everybody could tell I was the ink monitor. My mam did not care much about this as my hankies were always blue as I couldn't always gauge when the inkwell was full and I used my hankie to mop up the excess ink. My mam scrubbed my fingers with a nail brush - I didn't like this either so on the way home I tried to suck my fingers white. So I had a blue mouth too - a good job she didn't use the nail brush on my mouth.

I still had this burning ambition to be a shelter monitor. At home we hadn't got an air raid shelter. The man who lived over the road in what was Metcalfe's house was Mr. Ruecroft. His elder daughter Betty and I became friends. Mr. Ruecroft dug a big hole in their back garden beneath the concrete path leading to the back door and put some apple boxes in it to sit on and said we could share their home made air raid shelter. My dad always worked in ten o' clock at night shift. The air raids always seemed to be through the night but I knew dad would be alright because my mam prayed for the pit and the pitmen every night and she said if they won the war they would want the pits anyway. One night the siren went and my mam woke me up and we got ready in our siren suits. Mine was turquoise woollen material - the battle dress top and trousers were joined by buttons and the trouser bottoms were tightened by elastic, my mam's was navy blue and the trousers on hers were slack. We could pull them on over our nightdresses or pyjamas. I loved this suit and it was not so bad getting up in the middle of the night when I could put this suit on. Mam kept the insurance policies and valuables - I never found out what the valuables were - in a tin, inside a waterproof bag ready to take to the shelter. The tin was in case of fire and the waterproof bag was to stop the tin getting wet in case someone tried to put the fire out with our stirrup pump. Some bombs the Germans dropped were incendiary bombs and set buildings on fire. My mam and dad were 'fire watchers' and were issued with an arm band, a helmet and a stirrup pump. My mam said the stirrup pump had to be checked regularly so my dad used to clean the upstairs windows with it, he said this was the best use for it. It consisted of a foot pump and a hose which had to be used with a bucket of water. I wondered if it would ever put a fire out - I didn't think so but I enjoyed the window cleaning ritual. When I got in the way dad turned the hose on me and I laughed and laughed and got more in the way. My mam played war with him when I got wet, so sometimes she would make me watch out of the window and I would run from room to room as he squirted water on each window.

Another night the siren went and we made our way to the air raid shelter as usual. It was candle lit and I was half asleep. We settled on the cushioned apple boxes and my mother suddenly said, sounding terror stricken 'Don't move - don't move'. Immediately I was awake - alert- on my toes- yet I hadn't moved a muscle. Were The Germans here? Had my mam heard them on the concrete above us? Oh that damned illness I had had I couldn't hear as well as my mother, another thing I kept getting the same type of violent headache I had had then. 'Look under that box- a tail sticking out, the man over the road bent to get hold of it, 'Don't touch - don't touch' I was trying to work out the logic of this but I must have been too tired. We sat and stared at the tail and forgot all about the air raid - the Germans - the bombs dropping and the ack ack gunfire. I could hear my mother breathing. Billy, the son of the house across the road bent down then to get hold of the tail and I could hear my mother 'not' breathing louder than ever. Billy got hold of it and it crossed my mind we would have been safer in the house as we didn't have mice there. What if this house over the road was bombed and fell on us, in this shelter we would be buried alive. He pulled at the tail. Dead silence. Then he began to laugh, it was the long tail of a carrot. Billy was a bit of a joker. At every raid we laughed about this. The council built an air raid shelter in our front garden and that type was condemned so they built another in the back garden. I was obsessed with it. It was kept locked and I was forever asking for the key so I could air it and pretended I was a shelter monitor, but it wasn't the same. Apparently the council were building air raid shelters in the streets as these were found to be the safest. Joe, my brother in law and my sister had a child, a girl four years younger than me. They parted and Ena left her daughter with Joe and she stayed with his mother in Murton. He was Building Inspector for the council by then and he had this shelter built so Joan would be safe as she frequently stayed with us.

My parents were annoyed that Ena had left her child, my mam said she could have lived with us and Joan and I could have been brought up as sisters, but Ena said Joe had plenty of money and he was more capable of giving her 'things' than she was . I don't know where she lived as we never saw her but we often saw Joan and Joe brought her. To be separated or divorced was unusual and a bit of a disgrace then but I learned that Joe was having an affair with a teacher who taught at my school. My father went to the school and told Miss Wardell this teacher must not teach me, as her morals were nil. When told the reason why she said she thought Joe was this teacher's boyfriend. My father enlightened her and had it not been for the scarcity of teachers during the war she would have lost her job. The headmistress made sure this teacher did not teach me and so most likely averted a scandal. How times change.

Eventually I was ten and then I was given the job of shelter monitor of the bottom class upstairs in the Junior School. I was dying to know what was in the tins that I had to collect from the headmistress every morning with the blankets and leave outside 'my' class. Someone said it was barley sugar sticks and ovaltine and Horlicks tablets. The tins were sealed so I couldn't look in to see them as I thought they must not be in very good condition if they had never been changed. I never found out if they were and I did not like to ask in case I lost my long awaited job. One of the war slogans was 'Be like dad, keep mum' so I did.

When the snow came and it was very deep that year the shelter monitors had to go and dig the snow from the steps leading down into the air raid shelters. They were built into the ground on which now stands part of the Catholic Church, opposite a club and of course very close to the school. So off I went with the others carrying my spade to dig the snow. My mam would have had a fit if she knew because she always 'wrapped me in cotton wool' so I never told her. I often wondered why she did this and I think it was because my dad was old. He was older than anyone elses dad and he seemed wiser too. After shovelling snow away the air raid wardens who supervised us, took us to their air raid shelter which was a whole dug into the side of the school and gave us hot oxo with milk in it. This was the first time I had had milk in oxo. When I asked at home why we didn't have milk in oxo my mam said wherever did I get such an idea. I couldn't tell her, could I? I learned it through my experience of achieving my ambition to become a shelter monitor. When my children ask me what I did during the war I can tell them I was a shelter monitor.

I wondered if the war would affect Christmas and New Year. I knew all about the seasons, the months and days of the week, my father taught me. When I was six he said it was 'time' I learned to read the time so till I did, every evening he sat me on the kitchen table with his pit watch which had a big, clear face and painstakingly taught me the time. When the 'time' came to learn this at school I already knew it and the teacher thought I was very quick to pick it up but I wasn't really because it took my father a week to teach me and for weeks after he kept asking me the time, then he taught me Roman numerals.

I knew when it began to snow Christmas was not far off. I always got lots of toys, for a long time I was baffled as to how if there was no Santa

Claus I always received gifts from aunt Mary and Florrie from such a distance and my dad was always telling me how the snowdrifts at Sunniside and Tow Law were so much deeper than the one's at the coast and I thought they were deep enough.

Every New Years eve my cousin Jim (one of aunt Tans' sons) was our first foot. The pit buzzer always blew on the eve of New year and it was always a nice friendly sound then, in comparison with the times it blew meaning trouble. Jim was our first foot from when mam and dad came to Easington till mam died. Every New year's morning my cousin Eva's daughter Margaret and I, we were the same age, I constantly reminded her I was the oldest by two weeks and two days called at the house of my cousin Wilf and his wife Gwen who lived in Easington Street and got our New Years gift, a glass of ginger wine, a slice of fruit cake, an apple, orange and sixpence, then we went to my aunt Tans' who was Margaret's grandmother and we got the same again only her ginger wine was always red hot and we got another piece of spice and then rice cake and a piece of cheese and a half a crown, we had already had half a crown from my mam so when we called at Eva's our last port of call she would kindly wrap my cake up and together with all the fruit I had put it in my satchel. Margaret and I loved doing this. At every house we knocked at the door first and said,

>Knock at the door,
>Bottle of store,
>Please will you give us
>A New years gift
>The roads are very clarty
>My boots are very thin
>I have a little pocket
>To put a penny in
>If you haven't got a penny
>A ha'penny will do,
>If you haven't got a ha'penny
>God bless you

The door would then be opened and we would go in and wish everyone a Happy and prosperous New Year. We did this till we thought we were too old to continue.

CHAPTER TWENTY SEVEN.

In the dark cupboard under the stairs standing between my parents protectively embracing one another with me in the middle was the time that at nine years old I knew what the war meant to civilians. It was afternoon and the siren had sounded and mam had woken dad, he was in bed, because he was in night shift and things happened so quickly we didn't have time to go the a shelter that's why we were in the cupboard.

Rumours that England was to be invaded on August 15th 1940 had reached us in Easington Colliery. My dad said that the North Sea had been the German Ocean at one time and they were determined to get it back and this is the way they would come, by sea.

Every evening we listened to the news on the wireless and we would hear 'This is the Six o'clock (or whatever time) news with Alvarr Liddell reading it and we would sometimes hear the traitor William Joyce alias Lord Haw Haw interrupt by saying something like 'Germany calling, Germany calling this is Lord Haw Haw, and if it was announced that the egg ration would be one egg per person a week as it sometimes was he would make a comment about it and frequently mention a place by name. This was propaganda and reduced our moral as we thought the Germans must be very clever to be able to interrupt the B.B.C.

My mother said Hitler was sure to attack in the north as Lord Haw Haw had interrupted a radio broadcast to say the people of Easington would soon be eating the greyhounds. It seemed to my mother that this was proof indeed that he knew that we existed and hadn't the germans sunk the pit shaft and they knew exactly where we were.

It was happening. The invasion. Deafening noises of bombs dropping, ack ack gunfire and machine guns filled our heads and rattled our end terraced house. The ground shook so much that I am sure if the world had been flat we would have been thrown off. We huddled helplessly together in the cupboard under the stairs. In a despairing tone my mother repeatedly said "That's theirs". Her voice filled with hope, "That's ours a Spitfire". My mother knew by the eleventh month of the war the difference in the droning engines of the aircraft. We regularly were woken by the siren at night, a daylight air raid was unusual. If the raid carried on after midnight we were allowed to have the next morning off school. I always went to school because my father would wake me when he came in from the pit on a morning and ask me if I wanted to go to school or not so as I was awake I would go, any how I didn't want to miss anything that was going on. He always knew when he came to bank i.e. came out of the pit whether their had been an air raid or not, he didn't know till then as no one told the pitmen as they would be worrying about their families. The raids were mostly around us but were close enough for us to be alerted.

When the noises became distant my father opened the front door to see if the pit was still there. It was. But in the background in the clear blue sky high above the North Sea a 'dogfight' was in progress. The two planes looked like giant flies. We could see and hear an exchange of tracer bullets. One plane dramatically plummeted into our sea. The other flew south. The silent air was unnatural. It smelled acrid.

Shouting "I am going to our Tom's", my dad ran from the house. His brother Tom had a family of ten and lived near the pit where he guessed the Germans were aiming for. Mrs. Wilkinson from no. eleven Wear shouted in to us, "Mr. Hardman and Mr. Mullany have been killed". I was in the same class at school as Maureen Mullany, I had been to her birthday party. She lived in Boston Street which was an officials' street and the Hardmans and their two babies had just moved out of our street. The men were members of the recently formed Home Guard. They had been killed in the pit yard.

I watched open lorries acting as ambulances speeding up the main street to hospital. Somebody was holding another down. I could see blankets covering people lying uncannily still. I watched open mouthed from an upstairs window. "East has been bombed. Our Tom's son has been shot in the legs in the Trust field. There is a toilet sitting on a rooftop. The A.F.S. (Auxillary Fire Service) and police are there. It's hell down there". This was my father back after what seemed a short time as I in my horror stricken state had not noticed time. The death toll was fourteen. Many were injured. Three hundred were made homeless.

The plane which took a dive into the sea was the enemy. The British fighter plane had crashed into the sand dunes of Hart as it was called then, later known as Crimdon. The pilot was a white South African and he was injured but recovered sufficiently to fly again. I grew a little older that day. A week later the Durham Miners donated £10,000 for the purchase of two Spitfires for the R.A.F.

Sixty years later the drone of certain planes flying overhead can swing my mind back to wartime.

In 1942 I was eleven nearly twelve, I could not remember a time when there was no war. My mam and dad keep talking about before the war but I cannot remember much about it. The worst thing to me about the war is there are no Silver Link toffees which were my favourites. My mam says they are common and she doesn't know where I get my common tastes from. There is no ice cream either. The police took all the Italians away and they were interned in camps for the duration. Mr. Donnini had six or seven in family and they all except one daughter who was married to Charlie Passerotti were in the British forces and he was interned together with Johnny Equi and Matt Muscadinni and they all made super ice cream. Anyhow there was no milk for ice cream these days and food was rationed. Slogans such as 'Dig for Victory' and 'Potatoes are good for you' were well used catch phrases.

My mam has a friend who has a sweet shop so we always have plenty of sweets and chocolate which my mam gets when she visits her - she has a notice in her window 'No Sweets'......my dad pulls mam 's leg and says she is dabbling in the black market. Although we have plenty of sweets I miss going for them myself.

One day a shop had strawberry pop in and my mam gave me money to buy some, she said it will only be coloured water and it was - although I pretended to enjoy it. It was horrible. One of the things that was scarce was Virol, it tasted like toffee and was full of vitamins. I used to get a spoonful a day before the war. Something I did not miss was Sulphur tablets and Black Treacle. I was given this every spring to keep my blood pure. The tablets were crushed and put on to a spoonful of black treacle and I had to shut my eyes to swallow this. If I had a cold I was given a knob of butter, a few drops of vinegar, mixed with a little sugar and melted with and mixed with a small amount of hot water.

I love Saturday nights - every Saturday night I have a Mars Bar. With the first bite I try to eat the fudge part, then the chocolate and leave the toffee till last. I love toffee. The next bit I eat the chocolate first, then the toffee and lastly I roll the fudge round my mouth. I alternate the three and it lasts along time. My mam says you would think I never got anything. We listen to Jack Warner on the wireless in Blue pencil, Blue pencil while I do this. When dad teases mam about the black market he says what about all this tinned food, dried fruit, soap etc. she has hoarded. He asked how she would explain it to Hitler, she says she would bury it in the front garden if the Germans came. We have a song sheet with Run Hitler, run Hitler on - she is going to burn that if the Germans get here.

I have learned how to queue. On my way home from school if I see a queue I run home and my mam gives me money to queue. I have memorised the store number so if there is a queue there I don't need any money - I just join the queue and say the number. My mam says it is funny I only see the queues for fruit and sweets - I once queued for half an hour for a pound of plums and ate them all before I got home. My dad says it is a wonder I didn't run all the way home after I ate them.

At night we have a blackout and we have shutters up at our house made by my cousins. My dad puts them up as soon as it is dusk. Some people have black curtains or black paper blinds. Everything is pitch black out side as there are no street lights. We have the light in the kitchen fitted so that when the door opens the light goes out as it is an offence to show a light. I have a torch but the glass face is covered in brown paper with a very small hole in so if I am out in the blackout I can see my way.

One night on the way home from a friends house about six o'clock I was walking quickly and I walked straight into the post box which was situated in the middle of the path. I went home and had that terrible headache once again. Shortly after this the council ordered this to be moved into the side of the shop as so many people had complained of walking into it. This demonstrates how black a blackout can be. If there are stars in the sky or a moon it helps and we tried to see the way at night by the searchlights sweeping the sky for enemy planes, when we saw these of course an air raid could be imminent as sure as shot an enemy plane was in the vicinity.

One night I was going home from the Girl's Life Brigade meeting (I had joined this as soon as it started about this time) with about six friends - we were walking in a line stretched out across the road, arm in arm. You could walk in the middle of the road because there was no traffic. My friends were saying Mary this and Mary that when we heard a man's voice behind us shout Mary - Mary. I stopped and I half turned to the voice, not recognising it and in the pitch black darkness of the night we couldn't see a thing I said Who is it? and the voice replied Your grandfather. All my friends shouted Run Mary run and we ran for our lives. I did not have a grandfather - I never had any grandparents, all my friends knew this because whenever they visited their grandparents I volunteered to go with them. I loved to visit their grandma's and grandda's - they were very old - older than my dad.

After this an officer from the brigade accompanied us home and on another starless night we were making the way home and we heard a young man, we knew this by his voice, singing in the distance and as he passed us on the other side of the road it was lovely to hear his voice approaching getting louder, his voice echoed in the darkness and as his voice was fading away from us Mrs. Davison, the officer shouted Good lad. He sang South of the Border all the way through. Whenever I hear that song I think of that starless night and his voice coming to us through the darkness. He would never know what a comfort it was.

One day coming out of chapel Sunday school my friends and I were laughing and enjoying the day. It was a lovely autumn day. Every day without an air raid was a lovely day when I was a child. I was dressed in a blue double breasted coat, it was buttoned down the side and I had on a blue, felt, wide brimmed hat kept on with elastic under the chin. Walking down the steps from the chapel I saw a sailor in R.N. uniform standing in the ice cream shop across the way. I thought he was the most handsome man I had seen - I wish I dared go across the road and touch his collar for luck (a superstition) but I didn't dare. He had brilliant white teeth and laughing blue eyes shining from his very tanned face. I knew I would never forget his face and I would ask my mam to pray for sailors.

I did not know at the time but this was to be my future husband...

There was great talk at school of 'The Scholarship'. This was to decide who was to go to grammar school. I was told by my mam that Ena had sat the scholarship twice once at Sunniside and again at Easington and she had passed both times. Would I pass once ? Who is Ena and where is she? At last the great day arrived, SCHOLARSHIP DAY - the words were said in capital letters was here. For six months teacher Miss Hall had instilled into us we were THE SCHOLARSHIP CLASS. Usually four scholars or so went to Seaham Harbour Girls' Grammar School, the rest went to Easington Colliery Secondary School. I was always in the top three in class tests and was constantly being told by my class mates 'you will pass', but would I? My stomach continuously turned over and I felt sick at the thought I might not. There were eighty of us in two classes eager and hopeful.

After a restless night I must have fallen into a deep sleep and had to be wakened for school. A rare occurrence and I felt it was a bad omen. After breakfast I set off for school with 'Do your best' ringing in my ears from my parents. My knees were knocking, my mouth dry.

It was a lonely walk. There were houses, shops and people but few scholars as the rest of the school had the day off. Only THE SCHOLARSHIP classes and all the teachers had to attend that day.

At last we were seated in the classroom. Sitting down to attention I looked nervously around me, an empty seat in front, behind and at either side of everyone. I presumed this was to prevent cheating and copying. We wrote in pencil. Before we started the exam the teacher explained that if our pencil point broke we put a hand up, if we needed to go to the toilet we did the same. Teachers patrolled the corridor ready to escort you and presumably she was there to give help to any class teacher who needed it as she was not allowed to leave the classroom either.

We commenced as soon as the teacher said the magic word begin. I thought and wrote for what I thought was hours, not hearing a thing, my concentration was so intense. Eventually I finished the last question, raised my head and looked around. Everybody was writing furiously. I panicked silently inside. Had I forgotten something - I re-read the paper and did not correct one thing. I came out in a cold sweat. One other girl had stopped writing and looked very confident.

The teacher started a time countdown. At last she collected the papers in. We were dismissed. The next few weeks I tried to forget about the pending results telling myself I could not change any of the answers, they were either right or wrong. My future was in the hands of fate.

Paper was scarce so we had to careful about using paper at school. Pens and pencils were also scarce. There was no paint on the pencils either. This war affected everything. I always carried a pen knife as did many others to sharpen our pencils although we had a pencil sharpener in the classroom. It also came in handy for peeling a carrot I would sometimes buy to eat instead of sweets or fruit which of course were very scarce - that was a well used word .together with ration. It was unbelievable cakes could be made without eggs. My mam used to boil parsnip, mash it and put in banana flavouring so I would not forget the taste of banana. She also made cinder toffee and put bicarbonate of soda in to make the bubbles.

One morning the letterbox flap made a louder noise than usual and an envelope dropped on the mat. I knew this was THE RESULT. Spellbound I watched as my mother slit open the important looking envelope withdrew a sheet of paper, "you have passed", she said. At eleven years old this was my finest hour.

At Easington School we did not wear uniform, at the grammar school it was compulsory. I was soon kitted out with white blouses, navy blue tunic which had three box pleats, front and back from the yolk fastened at the waist by buttons on a belt of the same material. It had a square neck and two buttons on each shoulder and a hidden pocket in the skirt side. A navy blue blazer with the school badge on, a navy blue Burberry raincoat for bad weather, a school hat with badge and a brown leather satchel. Black flat heeled shoes were worn to school and sandshoes were worn in school so the clatter of children's feet was lessened. A gym bag of navy blue of course was needed for carrying gym kit and shoes. Everyone had to supply their own pens, pencils, rough notebooks, crayons and ink. A free pass was issued to travel by train.

By now almost everything was rationed and the rations were meagre. It could be as little as two ounces of meat, four ounces of sugar, two ounces of butter and two of margarine and one egg. Soap, blankets and almost everything was rationed. Everyone was encouraged to 'Grow your own vegetables'. Books of points were issued and these allowed tinned goods and biscuits to be purchased when available. Clothing coupons had to be used to purchase clothes. It was not easy task to fit anyone out for the grammar school moneywise or coupon wise. There was a black market in coupons and my mother used to buy clothing coupons from a woman with a lot of children, this was against the law but her logic was if she did not buy the coupons they would not be used as the woman could not afford to buy new clothing for her family but relied on the kindness of people to give clothing to her and indeed they were given mine that I had out grown. My mam also said this family could not have afforded all their rations if she did not help by buying the coupons useless to them. At this time family allowance and any allowances for families had not even been thought of, if you had a big family it was up to you to keep and provide for them.

The Ration book office was in an old derelict house at the village and to go for the ration books was an adventure as I had always gone to the village before under protest, my mother's protest. The old rickety stairs creaking as I went up them reminded me of the times I had come to the village with my friend Olga Martindale. Olga had an aunt who we visited who lived opposite the Kings Head, we had to climb a grassy bank to get from the pathless road to the house. Outside the street was a water pump where she got her water from. The house inside was very dark and mysterious. We were never content with just visiting the aunt but would go to Rosemary Lane and look at the doss houses where single men could get a bed. We were told this but I don't know by whom, probably Olga's aunt.. These houses were all demolished years later. Olga's aunt's house was struck by lightening and the whole street was demolished. We would walk past the old mansion opposite the village church which it was reputed was a land mark for sailors. Seaton Holme, the old derelict looking mansion housed workhouse men who were cruelly, I thought, dressed in bright blue suits so they were instantly recognisable as workhouse inmates. The old houses were so interesting with their outside toilets and rag and bone yards. We looked in the village witches house. She was called Blackberry Jane and we would watch her in the colliery pick cigarette ends up from the gutters and anything else she could find in the colliery back streets. She was a familiar figure and we children kept well out of her way and if I saw her going into our back street I made sure I kept out of the way till she was gone in case she cast a spell on me. My father laughed when I told him and he called her Blackberry Jinny. The windows of her village house were filthy but we tried to see into them, if she had seen us we would have run hell for leather all the way home and hoped she did not recognise us. My friend Patty Greenwell was being bathed by her mother in the bathroom which was downstairs with the window open when Blackberry Jane who had crept up the yard without them hearing thrust her head through the open window and said harshly 'Have you any coal?' Patty and her mother almost swooned and Mrs. Greenwell shouted 'No no go away'. They said they had never had such a fright. Actually this old crone owned property in the village but she was an eccentric. There was a mortuary at the village attached to the workhouse and as we walked passed if there was water running out as though it was being swilled out my imagination ran riot as to who was being cut up in there. It was great to be allowed to go to the village for the ration books and I never grumbled at this as I still enjoyed the old things in the village, the blacksmiths and the many pubs. Everything had such character and looked so old compared to the colliery. Sadly these places were pulled down or 'done up'.

The grammar schools had longer holidays than other schools and in September I started Seaham school. The boys went to Ryhope Robert Richardson's Grammar School, they travelled in the same train as us from Easington Colliery Railway Station but we were not allowed to travel in the same carriage as them, all the carriages holding up to ten people were separate. The train left at 8.25 a.m. and was never late. It brought mail and lots of parcels and there was always plenty of goods to load on to the guard's van. As so many men were at war there was a lady porter as well as men and a station master as it was a very busy station. We lived about half a mile from the station and when we got off the train at Seaham we had about the same distance to walk. We walked about two miles a day. The trains were driven by steam. The boys would sometimes trap us girls on the bridge across the railway at Easington by some standing at the bottom of the bridge on either side and as the school train went underneath we were covered in steam and soot. Imagine our faces and white blouses. We were not allowed to travel in the same compartments as them. Coming home they were already on the train when it pulled into Seaham station and when they got on at Ryhope would lie down in a carriage, when we opened the door a boy would pop up. We would run up and down the station platform with the same thing happening till we found a carriage boy free. The guard would be shouting, All aboard and blow his whistle and a boy would run from a compartment leaving it free and we would pile in at the last minute. This was fun for the boys. Mostly we ignored them.

The headmistress lectured us on our arrival and told us we must always wear our hats on the front of our heads not on the back which we thought stylish and we must not speak or have anything to do with the secondary school which was near. This was difficult as they would pass our school yard and shout, 'Stuck up and snobs' and things like that. In winter it was very hard too as they pelted us with snowballs and we were not supposed to retaliate.

The teachers were mostly elderly as a lot of teachers were in the forces as officers. I was in the A class and in the first year we were taught cookery and sewing as well as french, algebra, geometry, arithmetic, history, geography, art, english poetry, language, speech training and of couse P.E.and games. In the second year the A class dropped cookery and sewing and were taught Latin. We all belonged to a house, each house named after a famous seafarer as of course we were very proud that our school was associated with the sea. The school badge was a ship. I was in the Nelson house, the colour blue, the others were yellow, Collingwood, green was Raleigh, and Drake was mauve. We were given a badge if our deportment was good enough. I had a badge for this. We were warned by other pupils that the senior History teacher wasn't much good her lessons consisted of open your book and start reading where you left off. She was also noted for putting questions in exams on books that she had not issued that particular class with and we protested at this. This shows how the war affected one thing after another. Fortunately married teachers were brought back in to the profession, but the only married teacher we got was the music teacher. We were invited together with other schools to sing in Durham cathedral. I thought no chance for me, but the teacher took all of our class and I could say I sang in a choir in Durham cathedral. Mind you there were at least two hundred children.

By this time we did not carry our gas masks around as there was not going to be gas warfare. The air raids continued and no matter how long a night raid lasted we still had to attend school. One day we heard a school on the coast had been bombed. Places were never named in the radio news or the newspapers as it would create worry to relatives and the Germans would get to know the damage they had done. We knew that somewhere in Seaham had been bombed because whenever there was a raid we knew the direction of the raid by the searchlights scanning the sky and the sound of gunfire. We wondered and a few hoped it would be our school. From the train we saw it was an Infant's School. Our school had a window pane shattered. All windows were reinforced with net and glue to prevent bomb blast.

We had dinners at school on a rota system because of the rationing. The school kitchen was a short walk from the school over a level crossing and many a time we had to wait till as many as thirty trucks full of coal passed by. The dinners were served by senior pupils and I did this in my last school year. The school dinners were extremely tasty being cooked by local women. No certificates for hygiene or anything in the way of qualifications was required just common sense and a knowledge of good cooking. When you were not on turn for school dinners you had to take sandwiches or could get special permission to go to the British Canteen in Seaham Harbour. We never had air raid drill at this school although we had shelters between the school and the playing fields.

I was a member of the Girls' Life Brigade and despite the war we went to camp at Shotley Bridge and another twice at Borrowby in Yorkshire. We had social evenings with the village Lad's Church Brigade and I went to dances at the village and colliery church halls with friends. Jean MacManners and I when we went to the village church hall would go through the church yard to the fish shop for a bag of chips (fish was very scarce by the way though potatoes were plentiful) during the interval. In the dark this was an adventure as we would imagine we saw the tombstones move and we would run like mad into the hall and giggle.

My cousin Joe was called up and joined the Royal Navy. He seemed to have been away only five minutes, perhaps three months and he was due to be sent to a ship when he wrote to my aunt Tan and told her he had a heavy cold and was in sick quarters. He said not to worry as it was only trivial. Next thing he was discharged he had contracted the deadly tuberculosis, this was a killer disease at that time. He was sent home and was taken to Wolsingham Sanatorium and my mam and aunt visited him regularly taking goodies but I did not see him for years. I hate this war.

Then my aunt Mary died. I wondered if I had gone to live with her for the duration as she wanted if she would have lived, my mam said she wouldn't. She died in Newcastle Infirmary from cancer.

One of the boys in the Boys' Brigade died of T.B. Jean Mac Manners and I walked at the front of the cortege at his funeral paced by the funeral director. We carried a wreath each, behind us followed the hearse and then a funeral car with his brother, sister and stepmother and father. His mother had died of T. B. Then followed the boys, girls and distant relatives on foot. We walked from Paradise Crescent at the waterworks to chapel and then to the cemetery. Every man we passed took his hat or cap off and the women stood still. This was a mark of respect.

When I was about sixteen I joined the church centre which was a youth club. We paid two shillings and sixpence a year. There were no organised activities but it was a place to go have a drink of tea or coffee and meet friends. There were billiard tables and a table tennis room.

April 27th 1942 the Empire Cinema was destroyed by fire, a few years later when I was going to school the ruins were on fire again supposedly hit by incendiary bombs.

In January 1944 the miners had a one week strike and in the March the 450 putters decided to have a go slow for more pay. Men continued to have accidents and my father said that two men were barred in, that was his expression for saying trapped. When the Bevin boys were conscripted there were more men going around with broken limbs and hands and heads bandaged than I had ever seen.

Dennis Doninni whose father was interned was awarded the Victoria Cross posthumously and his parents and siblings were invited to Buckingham Palace to receive it. His father was allowed out of the prison camp for this visit. What a farce. There had been a protest in Easington when the Italians had been taken away as they were all respectable quiet business people who did a service to the community. War seemed to me at fourteen to be a bit of a farce. In my religious upbringing my mothert ried to teach me 'to turn the other cheek'. My father's teaching was 'an eye for an eye '. I tried to balance the two but decided my fathers way was the right one, anyhow I had his common tastes

I wondered if there would ever be an end to the war. I tried to remember the things I missed. There were not many buses on the roads, those that were dragged a machine behind them that was in the place of petrol which was scarce, they were said to be some sort of gas. Iron railings had disappeared, taken for the 'war effort'. I missed milk, it was rationed, eggs, sweets and all food. Would I ever eat ice cream again. Clothes, shoes curtains and so on had all to be purchased with coupons and money of course. Would the man who came round knocking on doors with his big wicker basket selling crumpets return. What about the scissor and knife grinder who came round the streets sharpening anything that was blunt with his machine he pushed and then pedalled to make it work. What about the man who called regularly with his tray of cottons, elastic, tape, pins and needles. Where was he?

Would the war ever end? I wonder what happened to the handsome sailor I saw that day.

CHAPTER TWENTY EIGHT

Money was not too plentiful and on a cold January in 1944 the putters at the pit despite the war had a one week strike and in the March they went on a go slow. The winters were very cold and we always had snow my father continued to tell me it was not so bad as Tow Law but we still had plenty and when the wind was blowing from the sea I was battling against it with horizontal sleet stinging my eyes as though it was full of sea water and cold enough to cut your face off I was glad I lived here. The blackout was almost lifted, the street lights were on although dimmed and we no longer were required to carry our gas masks. We heard about the sinking of ships on the news, remember no T.V. only wireless and of course through the newspapers. Limited was the mention of places. This was the second world war my parents had lived through and my mother continuously reminded me to pray for those in peril on the sea especially as we saw the sea every time we went into the street.

My mother had been asked by the police sergeant to give a home for a short time to a young police officer as he had been unable to find anywhere suitable. This was to be only temporary and my mother reluctantly agreed. He was such a nice person he became like one of the family and he was called up. One day he came home on leave and he got married on my birthday. It was my thirteenth and I was going to the Grammar school. I missed him when he went into the navy because he helped with my homework.

There were lots of rumours about a big 'operation' that was going to happen, we heard that lots of ships had gathered in the south of England, some had been called from as far away as the Mediterranean. My mother said she hoped this was not going to be another Dunkirk where Chris had been taken prisoner. We continued to hear about him through Mary. Then the news was all about an invasion into France and we had the Germans on the run with a massive loss of lives on both sides. We were grief stricken Sid Green, the nearest I had had to a brother had been killed. It was June 6th 1944 and it was D day. My mother was anxious about Chris and any prisoners of war. What would the Germans be doing to them - taking revenge - I wonder? I wish I could get used to this damned war, trouble is there was always something happening. My father said he heard the sailors in The Med had had it particularly bad and he told of how servicemen had come back from the Great War in 1918 shell shocked, gassed and complete nervous wrecks. I wonder what happened to that sailor I had seen with the tanned face and blue eyes. There was a song about the sailor with the navy blue eyes. We were winning the war but still everything was scarce and we were continually told to pull our belts in.

The winter was as usual bitterly cold but we always had plenty of free coal. Men were killed at the pit and on November 9th 1944 Mr. Jobling and Mr. Smith were barred in. There were Mining Rescue teams specially trained to deal with pit accidents of this type. One of my Nightingale cousins was on the Crook team and often called at our house when he was called to Easington. Fortunately these men were rescued. It seemed we were surrounded by danger near and far.

In 1945 Dennis Donnini was awarded the V.C. posthumously. My cousin Joe's health continued to deteriorate and he was home now. I still continued to go regularly to my Aunt Tan's.

May 8th 1945. The war has ended. There was to be street parties to celebrate. We did not have one in our street as everyone was conscious of the fact the war was not over with Japan. My parents said the time to celebrate was when our 'boys' were safely home again and my father wondered how they would fare in the future having known nothing but killing for years. I went to the street celebrations in Wembley and some girls got up on to the walls and sang in the dark night lit by lamplight and the twinkling stars in the friendly navy blue sky and I looked up at the full moon and I swear it winked at me and smiled mysteriously.

We had no celebrations at school. 15th August 1945 and the war with Japan ended. The Americans had dropped an atom bomb on two of their cities. 15th August 1945 I was camping at Borrowby once again with the Girls' Life Brigade when we learned the Japanese had surrendered. We had a huge bonfire and celebrated by singing round the fire.

What about Chris? He arrived home and we learned he had been on a long march from Poland to Germany. His feet were very sore. Mary and Chris were married at the Easington Colliery Wesleyan chapel.

Mary looked beautiful in her white wedding dress, Chris by her side in dark suit looking very thin. Both looked very very happy and indeed all the family celebrated their good fortune in their being together at last. All the families had helped with the catering as food was strictly rationed but the ingredients were found for a wedding cake topped with white icing. They bought a house at Trimdon Station and Mary lives there now, widowed but she shares with me the wonderful memories she has of their life together. She feels Chris has not left her but is always at her side. I am sure he is. He was a leading light in the Methodist Chapel at Trimdon and was leader of the Trimdon Male Voice Choir which was much in demand to sing all over the country. They had no children. They celebrated their golden wedding in 1995. Mary has since died.

After the war things didn't seem terribly different as far as rationing went. Young men began returning from the war. As I was getting a bit older I learned how to ballroom dance and went to the village and colliery church halls where dances were held weekly, also the Welfare Hall which it was said had the best dance floor in the country. I joined the C. of E. church centre which was a youth club where there were no organised activities but it was a place to go and sit and read, meet friends, play billiards or table tennis. There was not much money about and when we could afford to go to the pictures we went. We also met in the local ice cream shops at weekends and on fine Sundays went for walks around the Welfare grounds. The Welfare grounds were kept in immaculate condition being funded by the Miner's Union. It was here that the football games, the cricket matches, tennis matches and bowling games were played. There was never any shortage of players or spectators. There was also a children's play area. There were trees, shrubs and flowers in abundance with seats nestling here and there. I was sixteen and old enough to leave school. I started work at Binns' West Hartlepool in the office. I worked six and a half days a week. I went by bus as did most people as there were very few cars about. Very few could afford them. My cousin Wilf had one and he got married for a second time to a war widow.

One Sunday, I was sixteen I was in Equi's ice cream shop when who should come in but the 'sailor' who I had seen all those years before as I came from Sunday School. He was as handsome as ever but looked older. I was sitting in a cubicle with my friend Jenny when he came to us and said to me "If you are looking for Connie" (another friend) "I have seen her going round the Welfare". I thanked him and he vanished. I asked Jenny what was his name and she said Jim Bell. That night I met Jenny again in Equi's and we left for home at ten o'clock. Everything closed at ten, the pubs, clubs and pictures as well. We were all working so obviously had early mornings. My father used to quote to me, Early to bed, early to rise, makes a man healthy, wealthy and wise. Jenny lived in the opposite direction to me and as I was going home in the twilight of that pleasantly warm June evening in 1947 who should stop to speak to me but the 'sailor'. He was coming from the British Legion with friends. He asked me out and I refused. He was older than my other friends. He said "I know where you live and I will be waiting for you at half seven tomorrow night". I laughed and left him and went home.

Next evening when I finished work I got off the bus at Jenny's and told her also I asked his name again as I had forgotten it. She told me not to go out with him as he was far too experienced for me. Jenny was about eighteen months older than me. I wondered how she knew these things. After she said this I was determined to go out with him for one time anyhow. I went home, got ready and he was there waiting for me in the opening along the corner leading to my home.

We got on well. I learned since he was demobbed from the navy he had done a course in bricklaying. There were special courses put on for ex-servicemen to help rehabilitate them and to get them into the civilian way of life as most of them had been too young to have trades. Some became schoolteachers as their education had been interrupted when they were eighteen. He was working and was never short of work as there was much building taking place as all that type of thing had been stopped because of the war.

He didn't talk about the war. My mother and father always insisted on knowing who I was going anywhere with met him and liked him. We went to Durham and he rowed us up the river. We saw shows at Sunderland Empire and went to dances. He took me for a drink. Goodbye ice cream shops and the church centre I was far too busy doing other things. I met his family of four sisters and two brothers. There house always seemed to be full with their family alone. He thought my home was like a morgue it was so quiet.

We were issued with clothing coupons for years after the war until into the nineteen fifties. Nevertheless we were still fashionably dressed. My mother seemed to manage to have sufficient coupons to keep the three of us well dressed. My father regularly got his new three piece suit. Jigger coats were fashionable and were a short waist length buttonless coat. I had a costume or two piece suit of a mustard finely checked material, the skirt had three box pleats at the front and one at the back. Blouses were silk, satin or cotton. Another suit was of grey and blues shaded into one another, the skirt had three inverted pleats at the front and one at the back. When the 'New Look' came out I had a midnight blue coat which was almost ankle length, a dull turquoise dress with a grandad neckline and gathered skirt of the same length. The material of the coat was called velour I think and felt like velvet. The dress was a soft woollen material. I felt a million dollars when I was dressed in these. I had summer clothes of bright coloured cottons. Two piece cotton suits in white and turquoise blue and white and red and dresses of green and red. When platform soled shoes were in vogue I had a pair, brown leather with ankle straps. I was two or three inches taller in them. I was only five foot. My mother could never understand why I was shorter than Ena and her and dad. Years later I read my generation were shorter due to rationing. I had a mop of auburn hair, the colour was unusual and everyone remarked on my hair which was very thick, easily curled and could be put in any style. I wore it just past shoulder length, didn't go to a hairdresser but my mother cut it. One of my fathers friends said I was the only person he had seen go out three times in one day with a different hair style. I would part it at the side and wave the top and curl the sides and back, another time I would pile it all on the top of my head, I would wear it in pageboy style or plait a piece from each side and put it across the top and curl the rest.

Tragedy struck. My cousin Joe became very ill and died. Another casualty of war. We all knew that T.B. was a killer disease but we hoped a cure would be found in time to save Joe.

When I was eighteen Jim and I were engaged. Meanwhile the pits became nationalised, much to my father's dismay as he was no longer on piece work but everyman got the same wage no matter how hard or how little they worked. He said nationalisation made a lot of lazy men. My parents decided to sell the house and move to a colliery house which we did in 1949.

We moved to Wembley and I did not like this house. At this time the first electric washers were in the shops and there was a waiting list but I got one from Binns' and mother was one of the first to have one. She still scrubbed and boiled the clothes.

Houses were hard to come by and it was the usual practice to live with in-laws and save and wait for a house as it was easier to get a house when you married. We were married at St. John's Methodist Chapel on March 18th 1950. I wore a white wedding dress and carried a bouquet of carnations. Jim wore a pin striped black suit. I left Binns' and got a job in the Council Offices at Easington Village. Things continued much as though we were courting only Jim didn't go home he slept with me. On December 28th 1950 I had a beautiful baby daughter. We called her Christine Frances and were very happy. All we needed was our own home. When Jim's mother saw Christine she told me of the Gipsy who predicted he would be the first to make her a grandmother and he was. He was 27 years old and had two sisters his senior and Irene was eighteen months younger than him and Hilda six years younger.

One morning Jim got up to go to work on a building site at Hartlepool and my father told him there had been a terrible explosion in The Duckbill area of the pit. He did not know how many men were involved but it happened at the changeover of shifts so a lot of men were in the area. Jim's father worked in this district and he had said that it would 'go up in a blue light one of these days'. That day had arrived. We learned that Tommy Thompson a lifetime friend of Jim's had been late getting up for work and had run to the pit just managed to catch the cage down and ran straight into the explosion and a piece of coal blasted through his forehead and blew the back of his head off. Another man had slept in and missed the shift and all the men killed were his marras (workmates) and but for fate interfering and causing him not to hear the alarm that always woke him or did it not go off - who knows - anyhow his life was saved and I remember seeing him standing at the mass grave as it was being dug by a mechanical digger. He cried as the digger incessantly droned in the beginning of June clear summer air contrasting with the smell of the pit he worked in. A wife of one of the men who was killed had made his dinner not knowing he was already dead, she had gone to the gate to watch for him coming for his dinner after his shift and as was usual when a man was late you would see a woman waiting anxiously at a gate asking each man she saw if they had seen her husband. The fear was always there that a man was hurt or worse and no one had got in touch to tell her. The worst had happened to this woman. As she waited a neighbour asked if she had heard the news of the explosion. She had not and the managers and union men had not got around to informing relatives relying partly on the local grapevine. No doubt they were too busy organising the rescue which was their primary concern. Fortunately my relatives worked in a different part of the pit and were all O.K. I had at least twelve relatives working down the pit at the time.

Christine was very poorly with an illness called Borneholme disease of which little was known and there was an epidemic in the Easington, she was five months old. When Christine began to recover I took her out in her high pram for a walk. The colliery band was playing a funeral march in Seaside Lane following hearses of men killed in the disaster. The effect the disaster had on Easington was devastating. This was a pretty depressing time but Jim and I still had much to look forward to and continued to look forward to our future. I have summed it up the disaster in this poem.

EASINGTON PIT DISASTER.

Head bowed at the foot of the mass grave,
Atmosphere serene and quiet,
My mind zoomed instantly back to the past
Imagination running riot.

May, twenty nineth, nineteen fifty one,
Can you hear the clash of a gate,
As the unsuspecting pit lad checks,
His water bottle and bait.

He glances back at his home,
Unaware of what lies ahead,
Not knowing the echoing sound,
Is his swan song, unsung, unread.

Pit baths, change clothes, catch cage,
Travel rocky underground hills,
Eighty one ill fated coal getters,
Walk to death in the North Pit Duckbills.

The explosion rocked thepit,
Black killer dust, white hot hell,
To add to the anguish of Easington,
Two rescuers perished as well.

Jim, Jack, Tom, Bill, Joe,
Jesse, Peter, Bert and John,
George, Mattie, Steve, Fred, Hughie,
A few of the men that we mourn.

Names written on the memorial,
On the hill overlooking the sea,
Ensuring the disaster of Easington,
Is forever preserved in history.

Accountants are able to reckon,
Politicians fight to control,
Argue prices, rates and profits,
EASINGTON KNOWS THE COST OF COAL.

My mother was not well. She went to the doctors and he told her there was nothing wrong, she couldn't exactly describe how she felt except she didn't feel right. The doctor said he would take a lease on her life as she was so healthy. My father taught Christine all the Nursery Rhymes he taught me and she was talking before she was walking at one year old. She was well nursed and my Aunt Tan who we now lived near came every day to see her.

June 2nd 1953 was the day of the coronation of Queen Elizabeth the second. My cousin Wilf had bought a television and this is the first one I had known anyone have. His wife Evelyn invited us all for the day, she lived in Easington very close to us, to watch the coronation on the T.V. instead of listening to it on the wireless as we would normally have done and later we would have seen some of it on the Pathe news at the local picture house. I decided not to go as I thought it was a long time for Christine to sit still and I would rather take her for a walk any how. The weather was atrocious. The rain never stopped all day. As my father said "It rained yal watter". A few weeks after the coronation we had a day similar to then with it raining cats and dogs. Christine asked "Is it coronation, mammy". Evidently I had kept telling her it was an important day and for a long time she associated rain with the coronation. My father asked my mother if she would like one of these new fangled things and they went to the co-operative store which sold everything and bought one. There was no colour then only black and white but I marvelled at how when I had gone to the matinee at the Rialto when I was a child I had seen Merlin in the serial Flash Gordon look at a screen and see what was going on somewhere else and here it was in my home.

Aunt Tan was worried about my mother. One day she got up and we could hardly understand what she was saying. She went to the doctor's, no appointment was necessary. She came home and said the doctor told her she had had a slight stroke and she had to go to bed and he would come and examine her at home.

Sadly my mother's health deteriorated. Every day she was a little weaker and she had lost the use of something else. Her speech first, where was God I asked myself. My mother sang his praises and now she had lost the power of speech, for a while she could go out and about but always my aunt or I went with her as she could not speak. Then half her tongue was paralysed, her throat muscles inside and out so she could not hold her head up. Then she had difficulty walking. Jim and I bought a house very near, it was on the edge of an estate called Canada, the real name was Holmehill Estate. The address was 6, George Avenue. My aunt Tan helped Jim and I to clean it and we moved. Every day I went to see my mother and to do her housework, cooking and so on. Sometimes when she seemed to be worse, if that was possible, Jim and I would move back to stay for as long as necessary.

My sister Ena had to be informed and rarely came. In fact Jim and I had courted for two and a half years before he knew I had an older sister!! Years later I realised this illness was Motor Neurone Disease and the doctors must never have seen it as they were unable to diagnose it.

I was pregnant again with a much longed for second child. Margaret was born on 12th April 1956. She was a very placid child and my parents adored her too. We now had two beautiful daughters and the only thing that marred our happiness was my mother's health. Sadly when Margaret was sixteen weeks old my mother died. Again I had been hoping for a miracle which never came.

CHAPTER TWENTY NINE

We had to adjust to a big change. Between us we decided my father should live with us as my mother had requested as he was not the type who could look after himself and live alone. He would have fretted too much. My mother was his whole life. Everything he did he did for her. Besides Christine and Margaret would keep him interested. He now nursed and took Margaret for walks in her high pram and then he taught her all the nursery rhymes and sang her to sleep. Gradually we accepted my mother's death but I was very bitter about her illness. My friends all still had their mothers and I am sorry to say I envied them and begrudged them this. Very rarely we saw Ena who was married to Des Lister and lived Eston near Middlesbrough.

Jim bought a boxer dog, a beautiful bitch we called Sheba, something he had always wanted and why not. Life was too short to do without what you wanted. He also had started to work for Easington Colliery on the property repairing the houses. It seemed a more stable job than the building sites.

July 23rd 1960 we had a beautiful baby son we called James. My father asked us to put Albert in his name so we did and he became James Albert Bell. My father asked me to promise he would never go down the pit so I did. He also nursed him and taught him the same nursery rhymes.

Jim decided he could make more money bricklaying down the pit and so applied. He got the job and started to bricklay down the pit. People often wonder what does a bricklayer do down the pit. Well there were engine houses to be built, walls, doorways, concreting the new machinery into place as now machines replaced many manual jobs. There were no longer putters and hewers but power loaders who used machinery to cut coal faces. Machines loaded the coal on to belts to be brought from the faces. The machinery of the belts had to be concreted in. The machines were electrically driven. Offices were also built down the pit. The pit was modernised and known as one of the best and most efficient in the North East as well as being the biggest. It extended to six miles out under the sea. It was ironic that Jim was working under the sea.

Of course he had always been in a trade union as most jobs were what was called closed shops and if you did not join the trade union you could not work in certain places. This applied at the pit. Jim had been a member of The Bricklayers Union for many years but to go down the pit had to be a member of the Mechanics Union. He applied for a transfer. The procedure was to approach the union secretary and ask him to bring your name up at the next meeting, he would propose that you were to become a member, ask if there were any objections and then ask someone to second the proposal. Jim had a visit from the secretary Tommy Nicholson who told him someone had objected to him, saying as he had been away in the navy for five years enlisting when he was eighteen he could not have served his time and they were objecting. Well here was a turn up for the books, his memory was revived about the tin club. How could men who had had it cushy during the war as the mines became a reserved occupation after the war began, object to a veteran!! I was irate and wished this man or men into an early grave, not so politely as that. Jim took his papers to the next union meeting and threw them on the table, they stated his qualifications and also advised if he had any trouble with trade union members or in getting a job the War Office had to be contacted. Tommy said to leave it with him. Jim was accepted, the objection thrown out. Jim inquired who the objector or objectors were but it was against union rules to disclose this information. He had an idea who it was. Years later when I was compiling Past and Present I was looking through old union minutes when what should jump out of a page at me but the objection and the names of the men were Joe Black and Barney Mulholland who he had never suspected. The only reason these men had objected must have been jealousy and always people remembered him for 'being in the navy', otherwise what reason. We had three children and I think what these men tried to do is unforgivable. Perhaps my father's an eye for an eye was etched in my brain.

Jim continued working at the pit. My niece Joan had got married to Harry Anderson and her father still owned a plot of land in Murton and suggested Harry and Joan move to one of his bungalows in Hawthorn and begin building on it. He did and Jim worked for him as well as working at the pit, so he was working sixteen hours a day for a time. It was nice for me to have Joan near and we often visited each other. Easington council put so many obstacles in Harry's way that after building a street of houses he decided to return to Eston, Yorkshire - now Cleveland.

Jim was not well and the doctor advised him to work five days a week. I saw an advert in the paper for pupil nurses at the local Leeholme hospital that had once been the workhouse but was now a teaching hospital with seven wards, Men's surgical. womens surgical and gynae and geriatric wards. There was also a busy out patients department and an X-Ray department. I talked over with Jim and my dad the prospect of applying, seeing a way of making money and also doing something I had always wanted to do. They agreed so I applied and was accepted. My three children were all at school now. Jimmy was five years old. I started there in September 1965 and took to nursing like a duck to water, must have been something to do with the name (mine).

I had a phone call at work in November the children had been sent home from school because of bad weather and my father could not be roused. One of the dogs was in the house, the other a son of Sheba called Khan refused to bark although the neighbours were knocking and knocking. I immediately went home knowing something serious must be wrong as my father adored the children and for him not to be there was out of character. I arrived home, not having a key as there was no need for me to take one. Jim had been in the house when I left at 7.30 a.m and he would have locked the door when he went to work at 8.30 a.m after seeing the children out to school. He always spoke to my father before he went. Jim was not due home till about six so as this was about quarter to five the men decided to break the door down and found father dead upstairs in his bedroom. I found a note from Jim to him telling him he had got plenty of coal in the house for him and there was no need for him to go out as the weather was so bad. The snow was quite deep and it was very icy. That was the only morning Jim had not roused him but he thought it was a shame to disturb him on such a bitterly cold morning. My father had died as his mother had very suddenly and he lived as he wished to see Jimmy start school. Ena came to the funeral but after that we lost touch.

The next problem should I continue with my training ? We decided we needed the money anyhow so I returned to work in January 1966. I sat exams and passed very easily. I was a State Enrolled Nurse. The tutor asked me how I thought about doing a further years training to become a State Registered Nurse. I declined as this meant going to work in hospitals at Sunderland and being away from home longer.

One interesting episode was as I was going from ward to ward one morning giving the drug keys out - I should explain the procedure - every morning a nurse who was working on Out Patients had to collect the drug cupboard keys from the night sister and give them out. Every night every ward had to send these keys to the matron with a report of the day. I was frequently on Out Patient duty which I loved as every patient was different and all the most recent cures and operations were learned about and I loved learning. This particular morning Nurse Olive Barrell said 'See if you recognise anyone in this ward.' It was a geriatric ward. I went and spoke to each patient and I did not recognise anyone I knew. She pointed to a bed and said, 'That is Blackberry Jane'. Here she was cleaned up. Apparently she had been found collapsed and brought into the hospital and the nurses who had had to clean her up had had to have baths themselves after bathing her (not in the same bath I hastily add) She had also been found to have lots of pound notes concealed about her body. This was before metric money. After this I heard the council housed her in a bungalow in the colliery council houses. There were no old peoples nursing homes at this time. The years rolled by. Christine left school and worked in a chemist's shop prior to beginning nurse training at Cherry Knowle Hospital. She had passed her eleven plus and attended Peterlee Grammar school, Margaret was attending Wellfield Grammar School and Jimmy was still at Easington Juniors' and followed suit and passed as well and also was a pupil at Wellfield. Grammar School so all three had qualified for a place at a grammar school. We were two proud parents.

Jim's father had died when Jimmy was a baby but I was glad that my children had known some grandparents, not like me not knowing any.

We had also moved into a colliery house which was rent free and all repairs were free. We had decided to do this a) because there was a lot of subsidence due to underground workings that affected our house and b) we wanted to have enough money to help any of the children go to university. We saved and were quite comfortable with our combined wages. By this time I was earning as much as Jim and could never understand when the papers were saying the nurses were poorly paid when I was getting as much as a miner.

There was subsidence under Leeholme hospital and there were rumours about closure. We were all suspicious about this as thousands of pounds had been spent on upgrading and alterations. The government policy was to close small hospitals. I heard of a vacancy at the local Maternity Littlethorpe hospital where Ann and Irene, my sisters in law worked as domestics. I started work there in 1969 - 70. Leeholme closed a year later but one of the new extensions is still in use as part of Easington Council Offices which extended its offices to the vacant site. (the council offices were to be demolished in 2013).

The pits went on strike on 8th January 1972 for an increase in wages. No free coal and no pay from the pit but because I was working and we had some savings we were not given any monetary help. Jim decided to go down the cliffs to the beach and collect sea coal. Some men did this for a living, after scaling the cliffs with a sack full of coal he said "No more". The pit resumed working on 28th February with a rise for Jim of six pounds a week. Surprise, surprise Margaret and Jimmy had got free meals at school for the duration of the strike, the head teacher did not like means testing and said every child whose father was on strike should receive free meals regardless of whether the mother was working or not.

By now we had got an old Ford Popular car sold to us by Jim's youngest brother Tom for a nominal sum. By nominal sum I mean a set of plugs and all the car cost in the three years he had it was the petrol he used. Jim's two brothers Reg and Tom were helping him to learn to drive and he also went to a driving school.

Khan our youngest dog had died and his mother Sheba had to be put to sleep. We were very unhappy when these things happened.

Leeholme hospital regularly had social events and the matron had a yearly dance which we all received invitations to. We also went to the dances held by the Littlethorpe maternity hospital. We had full social and working lives.

Christine got married and had a gorgeous baby boy, March 1944, this marriage did not work out and she returned home to live. There was never a shortage of anyone to look after Stuart and we all adored him. Jim sold the old Pop and bought a Ford Escort in 1973. We would go out in it to such places as Lambton Lion Park where you had to stay in your car and drive through the park as the wild animals roamed freely. We loved this and so did Stuart he laughed as the lions peered in the window, Christine and Margaret would shriek with horror and Jimmy would laugh at them and make roaring noises in their ears. The monkeys would climb on the roof of the car causing Jim much annoyance while we enjoyed their antics. We would then go to the picnic area and enjoy a picnic. One day a keeper was calling 'Little Jody come on little Jody'. We were of course sitting safely in the car, the keeper explained he was calling the baby rhino, we expected a small tiny creature when this huge animal came lumbering from behind a shelter, it was the baby who looked as though it weighed two tons ! We had a good laugh at this.

The next pit strike was in Feb. 1974 and it was a repeat of the first and we used up our savings again. This one lasted four weeks. My fathers' words kept coming back to me 'No good ever came of a strike'. I did learn that savings that were used in a strike were never replaced. The day after the end of this strike Jim's brother Reg, wife and three children emigrated to Australia. Reg had left the pit before this. His younger brother Tom had also left the pit and worked in a factory, later becoming a supervisor. Violet married and had two sons, Hilda married and adopted a child. Ann and Irene did not marry but lived together.

Tom, Jim's youngest brother and his wife Val had two children and we often went with Val and Tom to dances and clubs. Val and I would have our hair done, mine up in what was called petals and Val would have her blonde hair long and curly. We dressed in the fashion of the time, just below the knee length dresses and the men would be smartly dressed in suits, shirts and ties. Val decided to go in for teaching so became too busy studying to go out very often and we began to go more regularly to the local pub and dances. I was enjoying my work in the delivery rooms and theatre. We had very happy moments and very heartbreaking ones too.

The pit was working regularly reaching and passing its target and a flag was hoisted every time the target was passed and the flag seemed to be always flying gaily and gloriously waving in the brisk north sea air appearing to be shouting as it fluttered I am power, I am prosperous. A happy atmosphere reigned over the life of Easington Colliery. Keep gannin Marra and wot fettle could be heard - greetings among the men and people were smiling as they went about their business.

CHAPTER THIRTY

Jim heard about a naval association it was the Twenty first Destroyer Flotilla Hunt Class Association 1942 - 1945 and he joined. We went to Portsmouth every year and met old shipmates. When they met it was as though it was yesterday but they had much to catch up on and had all gone different ways, none more different than Jim's. Everyone instantly recognised him by his voice and said how it took them three years to understand him. Nevertheless after a weekend with us Jim was not talking as they were but they were saying 'Why aye man' and using the word canny. One of the wives asked me what canny meant as I said we had gone a canny way out in the boat to lay the wreath which we did in memory of comrades who lost their lives at sea. I had said that the weather was canny and it was a canny meal we had and the captain was a canny man. I did not know I used the word so much until then!!

We became friendly with retired Captain Peter Dickens, great grandson of Charles and I wrote to him about our life as he was interested in what happened to the young sailors and worried as to how they would cope after their ordeals. Commander Warren another Captain of the Blencathra expressed the same anxiety. In one of Peter's letters he wrote suggesting (hoping I would not think this was presumptuous of him) I write things down as he and his friends looked forward to my letters - he read them to his friends -. He said some day someone would read them. If not now they would be appreciated later. I did as he suggested and as a lot of things came to my mind in rhyme - due to my father maybe - I write a lot of things in rhyme.

Commander Warren wrote to us one Christmas reminding Jim of a Christmas in the Med. off North Africa when the crew were all ready to sit down to a much awaited dinner when the alarm ordered them to action stations. A battle followed and the dinner was never eaten. They spent Christmas that year attacking and being attacked under heavy gunfire. War is no respecter of high days or holy days. We still keep in touch of the few who are left.

Jim was wanting us to spend more time together so when a vacancy came up in the Out Patients Department I applied for it and got it. Some of the clinics besides being Maternity clinics were the Gynae clinics that had been transferred from Leeholme when it closed. I had every weekend off and all bank holidays.

Christine, an avid reader continued learning, remarried and had a baby daughter Dawn. Margaret to our great delight passed all her exams and was accepted for Hull University. She qualified from there as B.A. with honours. Her subject was foriegn languages, French and German and she had spent time studying in France, Germany and Switzerland and always continued learning. Jimmy decided to leave school at sixteen and became apprenticed as an engineer at Durham Mullards. He never ceased learning and went to Hartlepool College and got many certificates to further his career.

A lot of pits had closed after nationalisation with men being transferred to long life successful pits. This was hardly noticeable as there were so many pits open. Easington pit no longer needed apprentices. We were still not too worried about this as our pit continued to produce more than its target and drew more than one million tons as it had done in the early days. This time the men were power loaders using sophisticated machinery costing thousands of pounds. Safety was a priority and the Safety Officer George Otterwell was very strict and rarely now a life was lost. Damp spraying was introduced to settle the dust and masks were issued- not used by all. It had long been compulsory to wear a hard safety helmet and metal toe capped boots. Some men had silicosis, pneumonicosis and many had bronchitis through the black killer dust. Men working side by side - one would have a chest complaint another would not - this was the same with deafness which was a scourge among the pitmen due to the incessant noise of the surrounding machinery in an enclosed space, This was an unseen illness Jim became deaf and his bronchitis worsened and it became chronic - men could apply for redundancy with pay until they were sixty five and a lump sum. Jim applied on the grounds of his health and was successful. I reduced my working hours too as some clinics were being transferred and there were rumours of the hospital closing. This was about 1981.

Our family were all doing well and we were happy. Then our happiness was marred by rumours of the closure of the pits looming ever nearer. The local feeling was not to strike about this but somehow or another the ballot was organised in such a way it was rumoured that Arthur

Scargill had his way and all the miners were on strike. The strike began in March 1984. The strike was a fierce fight for everyone. It was to last a year. Easington had always been regarded as militant and very union minded. The Tories were in government with Margaret Thatcher as Prime Minister who was thought to be unfeeling towards us, her Minister of Trade Michael Heseltine, true blue Tories both, unaware of the worries and uncaring of the pit communities.

At the Out Patients we all felt for the young pregnant women who were almost penniless as the striking miners were not allowed to claim any benefits. At the local club some of the wives organised free meals for the families using money donated from the local traders to buy the goods needed and begging from local allotment holders. The local shops suffered badly and one day a miner went to Marro's hardware shop to ask for another donation and he had not taken any money at all that week and had just received his water rate and council rate bills and was wondering where the money was coming from to pay and he said he could not afford any money, from then on he was hounded, his wife who never refused help to anyone at anytime was alarmed when she heard and immediately took some money to them and explained his 'bad day'. They refused to take the money. Her brother was Dennis Donnini, the local V.C. hero. Sadly Corinna ended up in a mental hospital, she fretted so much about the aggravation of this misunderstanding.

My friend Maureen Bishop, a nurse who I worked with for many years in the Out Patients, was a dab hand at organising transport for striking miners' wives who attended the clinic as they could not afford the fares and she either got the money from the Department of Social Security or saw to it that a girl who needed a lift was seen by the doctor just before someone who had transport and when the first one was seeing the doctor she would asked the second one of she would give her a lift. They never refused and Maureen would say to the first girl, hang on a bit someone has offered to give you a lift. If a child looked cold in its pushchair as happened one day a blanket would be taken from the cupboard to cover the child and so on. Warm and cold drinks were provided free.

One day a young girl was not her usual self. She was eight months pregnant, the procedure was a midwife called at the house of a pregnant woman to assess the suitability of it for the new baby. This young girl explained her house was very cold and damp and she had no coal. Her husband had been trying to dig some from the cliffs where waste had been burned from the pit years ago. Her husband was not a robust man and she was afraid her house would not be suitable for a new baby. I came home and told Jim to put some of our coal, that we could ill afford as we were giving all the time, into their coalhouse anonymously. He said O.K. but this is not the answer. So I phoned the local vicar, the Rev Tony Hodgson and told him of the young girl's fears. He told me he had no money left in any funds to help, but said leave it with him. The next day the vicar phoned me and told me how he had gone to the church after my phone call and prayed for a miracle and the next morning in the post was a cheque from a supporter to be used to buy coal for the striking miners. God moves in a mysterious way, he said.

Every day I looked at the angry looking grey sea and wondered when all this misery would end. Men had to chop trees down for fuel. It was an offence, who cared, the trees would grow again. The men became leaner and eventually it was too much for one man and he broke the strike and started to work at the pit. This caused further trouble and now we had armies of policemen marching down Seaside Lane. I sometimes wondered if I was still living in England. Pickets came from other pits.

CHAPTER THIRTY ONE

The strike was from 1984-1985. Our son was now married to Margaret Hearne who belonged Shotton. They bought a house at Shotton and had a baby son, Dominic. Another delight for us. We now had 2 grandsons and a granddaughter. Jimmy and Margaret came one day and Jimmy said he had been upset to see miners with buckets begging in the streets of Durham so when he and Margaret were doing there weekly shopping they filled an extra shopping trolley and gave it to a striking miner. Christine's husband was on strike. The miners would work painting houses, doing repairs, gardening or anything for next to nothing to earn a few shillings. Our daughter Margaret contributed to the funds when she could.

It was 5.30 a.m. August 1984 after a few hours of dead beat sleep I was awake again. The police, please let them have abandoned the siege. I eased out of bed, crept across the bedroom floor, looked through the net curtained window. They were still there, across the field, beside Station Bridge with their cars and vans. Hundred strong, high helmeted, blue shirted police intent on stopping the flying pickets bringing help to their marras at Easington pit. Waiting.

Beyond Station Bridge the North Sea was briskly pushing waves to shore in all directions. No uniformity. White horses haphazardly leaping. The August sun already hot sending flashing sparks off the water. The power of nature - watching.

One glance took in this familiar scene. I have lived in this colliery owned house in this colliery owned street for twenty years. My neighbours sea, railway, pit. I know the mood of the sea reflects the mood of the land. I went back to bed.

I lay worrying about the agitation bouncing from the sea. I listened to it. I was trying to get used to waking without hearing the clang of coal trucks racing across the Station Bridge. Noise that I had never noticed till it was not there. The whistle of engines and the warning hoots from the pit yard were my back ground music. Now hollow sound echoed. The bedroom window was open. A slight breeze from the sea rattled the catch. Alert. Alarmed. A muted noise ? Strange to me. I could n't identify it. I might as well get up. The alien sound drew me to the window. Thunderstruck I gaped. The field below was full of marching, striking pitmen. Voices silent. Their feet making the mystifying drumming sound, muffled by the grass. As they left the field for the road to the pit it did not empty. More men poured after them keeping the field full.

I hurriedly dressed. The gate slammed, my husband Jim, a bronchitic, retired pitman was already on his way to the pit. As I opened the gate he was shouting from the bottom of the street. "Hurry up you've never seen anything like this except on the tele". So I went. The pulley wheels were there in the background black steel silhouetted against the sky blue backcloth. Immovable.

The situation was a lone pitman strike breaker Paul Wilkinson (when changed around these letters turn to P.W. kills a union !!) trying to get to work in the pit yard. The police under government orders had been helping him day by day. Pickets were drafted in from all over the country to keep him out. Hundreds and hundreds of police from all over the country were detailed to get him in. Hence the police blockade on the main road at Station Bridge. The pickets outwitted them by leaving their buses at Horden and walking through the fields to Easington Colliery. A contingent of police were at the other end of the village too. Today they had got the scab into the pit yard.

About two thousand people were assembled. The noisy humming of angry voices vibrated through the crowd.

Suddenly there was complete silence. Hundreds of pitmen in casual shirts and jeans crowded at the top of the sloping wasteland that overlooked the pit gates. The police immaculate in their summer uniforms, blue shirts, well pressed trousers and imposing helmets with visors guarding their faces, holding a shield in one hand and a truncheon in the other in orderly rows like soldiers ready for battle, faced them. Power.

"Zulu, Zulu, Zulu", the pitmen began to chant. The film about a Zulu war starring Michael Caine had been on the tele that week. The scene was reminiscent of a battle in the story. Louder "Zulu, Zulu, Zulu". Then the stone throwing began. The miners surged forward. The police advanced to meet them. A police helmet was snatched and thrown in the air.

The situation appeared uncontrollable. Gradually pit lad after pit lad was arrested. The police were in control. The prisoners were bundled into police vans that came from nowhere. Sirens screaming they sped away from Easington to police cells. Well organised. Some of these pitmen were sacked by the N.C.B. and never employed again. They did not think that fighting to keep pits open would end in their being black listed. Irony.

The words of my father, dead a score of years came into my head. No good ever came from a pit strike. He had lived through the 1921 and 1926 strikes so I knew he talked a lot of sense. Every time there was an election, local or otherwise he quoted Churchill, 'If they won't work, shoot them' referring to the miners so if I am prejudiced it is inherent. The strike was about pit closures. My father worked in many different pits - Black Prince, Hedley Hope, Sunniside and a few more that had closed. Eventually he had settled in Easington a long life pit. He was sure he would end his working life here but he insinuated some would not, but he was also sure more pits would open as had always been the way when one closed. Coal would always be needed my dad said.

I had every reason to dread pit closures with no new pits in the offing. My home, food, clothing and nearly everything I own had been bought with money earned at the pit. The crowd dispersed. A few miners lingered in little groups. Angry but not knowing how to cope with the situation.

The summer was hot, I had never seen so many men walking about the place. Drawn to the pit some would stand and look up at the pulley wheels, still and silent. Others dawdled past, eyes downcast as if unable to look the pit 'in the eye'.

Savings were used up. Insurance policies cashed. The sea was unnaturally calm. The horizon invisible behind a moving haze of silvery dazzling mist which could hide a mysterious friend or enemy or oblivion.

There were many scenes of violence anger and emotion. Men were arrested for shouting to the police and other men were forced back to work through poverty and despair. One day there was a scuffle between a lone miner and the police among a crowd at the pit. He fell to the ground as he was being arrested, he lay face down. Some onlooking miners watched as though emotionless, others turned their heads away. The police pinioned his arms. No one helped him. This was the changing trend caused not by fear of being injured or arrested but by the overhanging threat of being blacklisted by the N.C.B. Me? I took a photograph.

The summer turned to autumn. The weather changed dramatically. The north wind was so cold it just about cut your face off. Sleety snow, gale blown from the North Sea tasted of salt. Fuel became a necessity. Many wood fences disappeared. The denes became bare. The young ones needed to keep their young ones warm. The trees would grow again. Coalmen toured the streets selling coal. Polish coal they said, some said it was Easington coal. I tried not to think how it was acquired as I bought it. All pitmen had been used to receiving a coal allowance as part of their wages and were unused to having to even think where household coal comes from, now they had no money to buy it.

A young miner from Seaham it was reported on the front page of the Northern Echo was fined £100 for stealing £1.80 pence worth of coal. In the same article a man, not a miner was given a suspended sentence for stealing £11,000 pounds. The pitmen were being victimised or so it seemed.

I was lucky enough to be working. Through my job I met a lot of pregnant girls. One day a young woman arrived at the clinic. Her baby was overdue. She and her young husband carrying a toddler had walked seven miles. They had no money for fares. Desperation made them do it. They did not walk home. My friend Maureen saw to this.

Christmas came and went. Everyone wanting to get it over with as quickly as possible. I overheard some young miners wanting to go back to work. Their fathers were talking them out of it.

March 1985, a strange dark cloud had been hanging over the sea for weeks, the water looked as though it was boiling and as though every now and again a huge rock was hurled from the sea dropping back heavily sending spray a mile high in the air. The mood was reflected on the land, the miners were restless. Some not wanting to give in. Others wanting to get to work to settle their debts.

The seeming endless strike ended in March 1985. I stood on the crowded pavement and with a lump in my throat watched the pitmen of Easington parade down the main street to the pit gates. Open at last. The colourful pit banners fluttered and flapped in the spring breeze. Next the colliery band playing a rousing march. Feet moving in tune, a thousand men in harmony. Not triumphant but unbowed.

During the winter a drift back to work started. Forced. Frost on the inside of windows, hunger, young families, penniless. Pride pocketed they began to return to work, reluctantly. There were debts to be settled, loans repaid.

Relief and frustration were on parade. Grim expressions. Union officials Billy, Alan, Bob, Dennis in the lead. Jack father of four, Joe with two, Keith with one, newly married at the beginning of the strike. Dull eyed, worried faces marching.

The shopkeepers came to their doorways. Suddenly the mood brightened. Pay notes to come. Bonuses to be earned. A marching man started to applaud the shopkeepers, then another until the whole parade and the spectators joined in. Shouting their thanks to each shopkeeper by name for their local support they proceeded. These traders had regularly given food to the soup kitchen organised by the women, also two thousand pounds in cash. One of the traders who got a special cheer was for George Mills a green grocer who had contributed generously. I hope the miners never forget the support they received. Clapping, marching, faster tempo, hop, skip and jump to the band. Appreciation shouted, all the shopkeepers too had suffered. Not a dry eye on the route. Retired pitmen, women and supporters wept, and me. No victory. The procession disappeared through the pit gates. It was over. The men were back at work. Pulley wheels turning, engines hooting. Easington was alive. Mining coal. The sea was running busily up the black sandy beach with little white horses riding uneasily on the waves. Easington was back to normal. Uneasily? If anything was gained from the strike I have not heard of it. My fathers words, a pitman for more than fifty years echoed in my ears.

CHAPTER THIRTY TWO

Nissan a Japanese car firm planned to open a plant at Washington, Tyne and Wear. Our son decided to apply. He was doing well where he was and at twenty four was assistant maintenance manager but he was ambitious. He thought he was too young as young men but a shade older were advertised for. He got the job and in no time at all was travelling to and fro from Japan. Margaret became a schoolteacher. Christine was busy bringing her two children up.

Around us pits were closing. Men were coming here to work from the closed pits. Some moved here, some travelled. A lot of houses were empty and boarded up.

Eventually in October 1992 Michael Heseltine announced that Easington Pit was to be closed. Redundancies were arranged but what was needed was work. The pit closed in 1993 with many disgruntled feelings. It was generally felt that this was a punishment meted out by the government to the miners and it seemed Arthur Scargill had helped to close all the pits.

At about this time I was noticing at work that whereas a few years earlier married women were booking in to have their babies in hospital, the trend was changing and there were more single women booking in. Whereas at one time it had been a rarity for a single girl to attend the clinic now the rarity was a married woman. The hospital had been expecting closure for some time and it happened and all services were eventually transferred to Hartlepool. Just before this I had not been too well and retired.

I have not mentioned pets that we had after Jim retired. He bought a beautiful boxer bitch Sheba and I decided I would like a little dog so we bought a tiny Jack Russell we called Jody after the huge baby rhino. After Sheba died at twelve years old our son and his wife gave us a handsome boxer pup we called Max. Sadly he began to take fits at three years of age and he had to be put to sleep. Eleven months after this Jody had to be put to sleep due to cancer in her old age. We decided to have no more pets, as we could not take them for walks and exercise them as we used to. We missed them passionately.

The colliery houses were sold off and we bought ours for £3,750 and paid for it with our savings. We had already had an extension kitchen added as we knew we were going to buy this house where we had experienced much happiness. We had very good next door neighbours Nan and Ted MacManus who like us had three in family, sadly Ted died. Later their elder son died. We had other good neighbours too. Most of the people in our street bought the houses. There were only three rented out.

Jim had a pension from the War Office for his deafness as it was discovered that his hearing impairment was due to the deafening sounds of the guns all that time ago which caught up with him in later life. It has also been ruled that miners can apply for compensation for bronchitis.

Easington pit was demolished immediately after the closure announcement. At the moment plans are being discussed as to what to put on this huge site. Some shops have survived and some have closed. Shops keep opening and closing regularly.

When you go shopping now there are many strangers. There are complaints as to the type of tenants being allowed to live here. There are some bad landlords owning some of the houses.

We have had a new Primary School built to replace the old one which cannot be pulled down because there is a preservation order applied for secretly put on it that no one knew about. A building firm has bought it for a song the rumour goes. A lot of the streets are looking derelict.

Resident's Associations were formed and together with the local councillors are pulling the place together again. It is hard work, funding has to be applied for and many meetings attended. There has always been some crime but we always knew our own criminals but when the strangers arrived crime increased. Crime seems to be on the decrease at the present time.

I can only recollect two murders in Easington. One in the sixties when a man was kicked to death up Canada, Holmehill Estate. Four men were charged and were set free. The second a young man 'accidentally' killed his baby son aged six weeks in the B streets. He is serving life for murder. His wife was not charged.

Suicides, one in the thirties a man committed suicide on the railway line, another three did this, one in the fifties, sixties and nineties as far as I can remember. A man hung himself in the dene another behind the pantry door, another in Walter Willson's shop where he was carrying out alterations. Sadly my sister in law hung herself in August 1999. She did not appear to have any reason to do this other than she was depressed and very severely mentally ill.

Jim's oldest sister Violet and her husband are now dead, as is Hilda's husband. Reg returned from Australia alone and got divorced, remarried, divorced again and is engaged to be married again.

My elder daughter Christine is secretary of the North and Southside Resident's Association and is very involved with the regeneration of Easington. She attends night classes for computer learning, business studies and continues learning. Margaret has been married and divorced and is Head of Department of Languages at Hele's Comprehensive School Plymouth. She frequently goes abroad to France and is always going to various courses to do with education and continues learning as well as teaching. Jimmy is Senior Engineer with Nissan. He is currently gaining certificates in deep sea diving and continues to learn new skills. They are all computer literate.

Stuart our eldest grandson is chief in the scanning Cardiology Department at Carlisle Hospital. Dawn is working for a telephone answering company. Dominic is working at Nissan. Rebecca is still at Wellfield Comprehensive School.

Me, I am learning Computer Skills and of course writing. I paint in water colours and have learned the art of Pergamano which is cutting, embossing and painting pictures on parchment paper. I usually make these into greetings cards and write the verse myself. Jim keeps the yard looking very pretty with flowers and plants and sees to the maintenance of the house.

We have seen many changes. The greatest invention we agree is the computer.

I look back and remember how I saw Easington being created and then almost destroyed. I look forward to seeing it rebuilt. One of the traditions long gone was at a wedding a crowd mostly children would gather outside the bride's home and as she and her father drove away her father would throw coppers from the car window and the children would scramble for the money.

On a New Years Eve you would see a man waiting outside every house waiting for the pit buzzer to blow midnight hour and they would enter the house and then the visiting of each others would begin. Can we trust no one to take anything from our homes now or will they be sizing up the house. My brother in law, Tom had his milk stolen this morning, it has happened before. It seems school children from the local comprehensive have taken it as he found the bottle near the school. The only children to pass his house come from the neighbouring private estate. Is anyone above suspicion and how can we revive our traditions? Another tradition is that this year the November 5th bonfire night display held by the Parish Council has been postponed till February 2000 !! How can you postpone the burning of Guy Fawkes.

My wishes for Easington are to see the greedy landlords get their comeuppance - punishment- an eye for an eye some way or another.

Children to be educated in the home about right and wrong.

To see it become a peaceful, historical, pretty seaside come fishing village where people would come for its tranquility and friendliness.

The pit site to be well laid out.

Some of the houses to be used as private coastal holiday homes for city dwellers who would come and inhabit them at weekends and holidays.

Cleanliness every where.

A happy and prosperous and safe feeling atmosphere.

The regeneration scheme to be successful.

I hope you have enjoyed reading about the life of Jim and I in the twentieth century. The most important thing in our lives have always been our three children and grandchildren.

I intend from now on to write a weekly diary and yearly put it together for the next few years.

The 21st Century

CHAPTER THIRTY THREE

NEW YEARS EVE 1999

Instead of a noisy celebratory night things were very quiet in Easington Colliery. I heard later that the pub, there is only one that is Devlin's which will be forever known in its old name The Trust, and clubs were very quiet. It appears everyone decided to stay at home and watch Tele. We did. We saw the fireworks celebrations in Newcastle and allover the world. There has been controversy as to which year is the end of the twentieth century, 1999 or 2000. All nations have opted for 1999.

I had suggested to Rick Burnip (parish and district councillor) some time ago that we celebrate the new century with a firework display on the pit site but that came to nothing. Jim and I talked of the past. What should and could we have done to change things. We talked of the year 2000 and what it would bring. More doors opening showing improved conditions for all.

Some important dates. : We will have been married fifty years on 18.03. 2000. The old saying Tempus Fugit – well time has flown for us.

I will be seventy in October. Jim says he cannot imagine I am seventy. He still thinks of me as twenty-one.

Christine will be fifty on 28th December 2000. She looks about twenty-one. One thing we would not have changed is our three children. I wish we could have done more for them. However they have all done well and we are proud of our family.

Midnight. We are in bed watching the Tele. The phone rang once, twice, three, four times and more. Our children and grandchildren all thinking of us at the beginning of the new millenium. We had been talking of them and hoped for their futures to be full of blessings of every kind and success in all they do.

Preparations were soon in hand for the golden wedding celebrations. It was decided that we would go to St. John's Methodist Church to have our marriage blessed. We would then go for a meal to the Half Moon at the village for a meal. There is nowhere in the colliery suitable. We could do with a good class restaurant in the colliery.

I bought and hung new orange and yellow curtains in the house to represent gold. The only fly in the ointment Margaret could not come from Plymouth. Jim kept saying, "If only Margaret could come it would be perfect". It would. The weather of course is unsettled but we have always said if you put everything off because of the weather you would not do much.

Christine went with me to choose a dress. It was green, with swirls of pale yellow and made of floaty material. I bought a three quarter length jacket to go over it. I ordered a spray of orchids for Joan and me. For everyone else I ordered yellow carnation buttonholes backed with gold leaf. One for the men and two for the women.

Dominic, Jim's and Margaret's son is not well. Henuchs' has returned. Jim and I decided that if he is not able to come to the celebrations we would cancel it. We are very worried about him. Fortunately he got over this relapse and everything went as planned. If only Margaret was coming. A special guest our best man and his wife Joan are coming.

There has been much hustle and bustle. We had thought of hiring a minibus but there are enough cars in the family to ferry everyone. Jim's sisters and brothers are coming as well.

Friday evening March 17th 2000. There is a commotion as the back door flies open . Christine comes on all excited and I think Stuart and Brian (Brian often stays at our house and is a friend of Stuart's). Look who's here. Margaret with flowers and a bottle of champagne! Perfect.

At last the day is here. The weather is warm, sunny and mild. The best spring day we have had this year. The daffodils are blooming on the grass verge in front of the house. The air seems to be filled with happiness. The birds are singing. A chorus especially for us on our special day. The sky is a beautiful clear blue.

We are going in Stuart's car. It disappears. I think they are 'doing it up' to take us to church.

Time to go. Jimmy says, "Mam, dad, your transport is here". Where is Stuart's car? A white Rolls Royce is at the door with chauffeur in uniform!! He took us to church and we learned later our children had conspired to arrange this and shared the cost. We went into church and walked down the aisle, arm in arm this time. Jim had recalled the first time and said he would never forget looking round and seeing me on my father's arm walking down the aisle to become Mrs. Bell. I digress. As we walked down the aisle a tape began to play. When you were sweet sixteen, when first I saw you on the village green, I love you as I loved you when you were sweet sixteen. We continued to walk down the same aisle in the footsteps we had trod fifty years before. Fifty years older than the first time. Very emotional – I saw Joan take her hankie out. We had stood at the altar the first time. We sat this time. Tom videoed the service. The minister, the Reverend Alf Waite gave a brilliant service. He had a younger learner minister with him who read part of the lesson. The readings were from Genesis chap1. 27, 28. 1st John chap 4 :16 Psalm 127:1. Hymns 566 and 13. 'Now thank we all our Gods with hearts and hands and voices' was one and the other 'Praise my soul the King of Heaven'. Alf spoke well of us and our family and the fifty years. During the service he said it is time for another tape. "O how we danced on the night we were wed, We vowed our true love though a word wasn't said, The world was in bloom, There were stars in the skies, Except for the few that were there in your eyes, Angels were singing a hymn to your charms, Dear as I held you so close in my arms, Two hearts gently beating and murmuring low, My darling I love you so." (Have you tear in your eye dear reader). Jim took hold of my hand. It was as though he was singing to me. It was wonderful. People were waving to us as we stood on the church steps and had photos taken.

The Rolls Royce took us to the Half Moon with Jim waving from it saying he felt like royalty being driven through Easington in a Rolls. Another surprise when Christine, Ray, Stuart and Brian had disappeared they had been decorating the Half Moon with balloons and banners.

On arrival everyone was greeted with a drink of their choice. We ended the meal with champagne, cake and speeches. Jimmy had helped me organise the Half Moon menu. All the family had been so busy. It was a day of wonderful surprises

Our Three children made a speech as well as Reg. and our best man Bobby. Then Jim, it was all too much for him emotionally. He broke down during his speech and I finished it off for him.

A wonderful day. Jim said he enjoyed it more than the first time round as we had our children and grandchildren with us.

CHAPTER THIRTY FOUR

We had met a lot of people in the last century. I had written to whom it may concern at Durham and suggested the have a literature festival. The outcome is Durham Litfest and I was given a garland of honour for this together with Denise Robertson, a writer and the young lady who organised it.

One day about 1990 we had been to Peterlee. It was a Sunday, very quiet on the roads. As Jim drove down Seaside Lane to our house a car followed us. As we stopped in front of our house this strange car stopped. A friend I had met through my writing got out of the car and opened the passenger side. The friend Alex McAteer said 'Here is a lady who would like to meet you'. I thought it could not be- was it her double – it certainly was. It was Princess Helena of Romania! She had read my pit poetry and wanted to meet me. From then on they were regular visitors. The Princess Helena and her husband separated and she moved away. We often spoke of her and wondered where and how she was.

Summer 2000 came, Jim and I went to Margaret's for our holidays in Plymouth. How we enjoy that. I love Devon and would like to live there. Jim is not so sure as his roots are firmly placed here. I would not have dreamed of it but Easington is looking so dirty, unkempt, graffiti everywhere and the derelict houses that I have to pass to get to the main street are a depressing factor. The days I go out and meet people who talk to me and hearing of plans of demolition help me get over this dispirited feeling. It did not help that we had two conifers that had stood and been fed and nurtured outside our back door in the yard together with garden ornaments were stolen. These people will never have anything but trouble in their lives from now on.

Have I mentioned that the great-granddaughter of the first man to be killed at Easington pit and I have been corresponding. She got in touch with me through an article, which appeared in the Northern Echo, which called me the local historian. She sent the letter to Durham and it found me and we have written to each other ever since.

I had a phone call from her, Margaret Sutcliffe, 'Can I come and visit you'. I said of course, thinking the phone call was from New Zealand, when. She said 'Now I am in Peterlee'.

Sure enough she arrived minutes later and we got on like a house on fire. She was staying at Peterlee with David Tate and his wife. David and I, it turned out, had gone out together before I had met Jim. Life is full of co-incidences and I love it. Unfortunately I could not remember having gone out with David and I felt embarrassed at not remembering him. Eventually I recalled he had been a member of the band and vaguely recalled his face as a young man. We all went out a few times. We found out a few things more about Margarets' ancestor and David took us all out to lunch at beautiful old Ramside Hall near Durham as a thank you for helping Margaret find out as much as possible about her great-grandfather. We managed to find out he was buried in Easington Village cemetery together with his death certificate and the number of his grave. I had always been convinced he was buried in the village as even though so many historians had said he was buried at Kelloe. I had also traced Margaret's other great-grandfather to Low Grounds farm in Easington which unfortunately was demolished to make way for a timber yard at the pit. I gave her lots of maps with it on.

The time came for her to return to New Zealand all too soon.

We have a resource Centre in Bede Street, which houses offices and lots of interesting things are to be learned there. Meetings of various kinds are booked there. Computer classes, Language courses, Health Teaching, photocopying and so on are there too. If you have a complaint or a query it can be answered there. If they do not have the info they find in for you. Also there is a small library for no charge. A proper community place. Pete Smith who works there is very keen to get a Residents Association Newspaper going. Christine works there too.

During the summer after Margaret had gone back to New Zealand a pit cage was put on the pit site. A service was held to mark this event. I wrote and told Margaret of it. I had felt the presence of her great-grandfather who had been frozen and preserved in the pit shaft for four years all those years ago. I told her I felt as though I was her representative there as well as for myself of course. She replied how she liked the thought of this.

White Lea Farm is accessible by walking to the top of the pit site. I went with Christine to an open day there held on a Sunday. It reminded me in a small way of my aunt and uncles farm at Tow Law although theirs was very much bigger but my uncle Bob used to visit this farm with his horse and cart in the twenties and thirties and maybe before for all I know. It is planned to make this into a working organic farm with educational visits for children. On the day there was a storyteller in a tent telling a story I had told to Taffy Thomas, story teller many years ago. A man member of a folk group told me he had been at a festival in the South of England when he heard Paddy say, 'I am going to tell you a story told to me by Mary Bell'. He said he was amazed. Anyhow I ended up telling this storyteller at the farm another story on condition when she repeated it she said I had told her. When next I saw Rick I said I thought this was a good place for a wedding as you can get married anywhere now. Also I said it could be used as a reception area for a wedding, plenty of room for a marquee. I could just see a bride riding in a carriage and pair up the hill to the farm. He laughed. I mentioned this to Dawn, my eldest grand-daughter that I thought this would be a fairy tale place for when she got married and she said, 'Gran that is not one of your best ideas'.

Jim wants to get another dog. Lots of people have been saying to me that they have not seen him for a while, how is he and so on. I realise he does not go out very much at all and if we had a dog he would be out on the field with it at least once a day and more in good weather. I feel mean about not wanting another dog. I have my computer, painting and other hobbies. I go to classes for computing and French too. So we are going to get a Jack Russell pup. Jim saw an advert in the Northern Echo someone has pups for sale in Kirk Merrington and son Jim is taking us to see them and guess what we bought a dog pup as all the bitches had been sold. There was only two left. I wanted the smallest in the litter and it was still there. He is beautifully marked and it has done Jim good to have him. He soon grew and has probably outgrown the rest of the litter by now.

Turning of the Tide had a night called Sea of Light to celebrate a project to clean the beaches. There is a lot more to be done but this is the end of the first part. In preparation Christine and I went to a class where we made a large lantern each and the couple who taught us gave us another one each. We felt a bit odd walking from the Youth Centre (where we made them) down Seaside Lane carrying these huge white lanterns. People were asking where we had made them and why. When we told them they were for a celebration night on the pit site they were either bemused or intrigued and some said they would have come with us to make a lantern if they had known.

We could do with more publicity for events that go on in Easington. The evening it was held was dark, the sky was a midnight blue studded with silver stars. It was not cold. I had phoned my friend Theresa Caygill from Horden and she came on a free bus. Special buses came in from other former pit villages too. The site was floodlit and held roundabouts, hot dog stalls, a marquee with info of the project and the stage it had reached and the next thing to be done along the coast, and hundreds of people. A local radio station broadcast a programme about the event with lots of music in between updating listeners to what was going on. We were told where and when to rendezvous with our lanterns and together with other grownups and children we moved in a procession round the site. Our lanterns shining and swaying in the darkness like beacons heralding a new enthusiastic beginning of a new dawning for our Easington we paraded proudly to the front of the crowd.

Searchlights played criss crossing across the calm night sky lighting up the coastline and the sea reminding some of us oldies of the war years when the searchlights would catch a plane in its beam and us then young ones would wish for our guns to shoot the enemy plane down into the sea. People like my mother would be praying for the safety of the crew of the plane.

Then the fireworks began. They were lit at Seaham, Crimdon at the same time as Easington so the sea truly was a Sea of Light. Displays of red, white, blue, pink, purple, green and every colour flying through the clear midnight blue sky seeming to shout to the world 'We are still here. We will survive'. It was a most enjoyable evening with everyone in a good mood and I realised that if we all worked together and kept together we could keep our community spirit that we have always been noted for. Most of Easington was there as well as people from local communities.

I saw Rick. He said "Well Mary you've got your fireworks after all".

CHAPTER THIRTY FIVE

October 11th 2000. My seventieth birthday. Christine would have liked to have a party in the Officials' Club. She suggested that my old friends from workdays could be invited as well as family and friends of course. I was not in the mood for this besides a Thorpe reunion was arranged for November and I did not want to pre-empt this. I decided to have a quiet evening at home with all the family which is what I love, my children and grandchildren all together with us. Unfortunately Margaret was not able to surprise me this time but phoned which was second best thing.

On the morning Christine called with chocolate cake and champagne for breakfast which was a good start to the day. Jim keeps looking at me and still saying "Mary I cannot imagine you are seventy". Neither can I.

On the Saturday evening we had our family party. Jim's wife Margaret catered, she is very good at this and is a wonderful cook. I was overwhelmed with the presents from all. I will mention only one as you might share with me in watching it. My grandson Stuart and friend Brian had a star named after me so for eternity my name and star will be around. The star is at the head of Pegasus, the number Pegasus RA 22h 13m 34.26s D05 08' and that star is registered and will permanently be known as Mary Nightingale Bell and can be seen shining brightly October to December.

In November I had a phone call from my fiend Maureen Bishop there was to be a reunion of Thorpe Hospital Staff and when she called at the doctors' surgery a young nurse said she had been given a list of people to get in touch with m, did she know any of them. She said she and I were top of the list and when I said perhaps they were in alphabetical order she said no they were not. We went and had an enjoyable nostalgic evening with some people missing and others sending apologies and it was such a success it is to be arranged next year again. I wish some of these things would happen in the summer. Sadly this did not happen again.

Christmas 2000. We were all together again. Margaret came by car from Plymouth. She does not usually travel so far by car in the winter as the weather can be so changeable with snow and ice hovering ominously. Unfortunately Margaret planned to go home on the 29th the day before Christine's birthday party. She did stay for Christine's birthday on the 28th but the party booked at the Officials' Club was to be held on The Friday evening which was 29th December.

On the 29th, what did I say about the weather, snow and ice had us weather-bound. Margaret was forced to stay for the party. Fate or what- I believe in fate. We slipped and slithered to the party on the night at 7p.m. wondering if many people would venture out on such a treacherous night. We need not have worried. The place was full. The buffet meal was scrumptious – the stewardess catered and she did well. The DJ was very good. A lot of people danced and everyone sang and laughed and had a jolly good time. So much so that we forgot about cutting the cake. Christine saw that everyone got some cake later. I have not seen so many people enjoy themselves together for a long time. We were the old, middle aged, young, younger and teenagers. It was great for Jim and I as once again all our children and grandchildren were together. Jim's sisters could not attend but his brothers and their partners came. Lots of Christine's friends were there and told me for weeks afterwards what a great time they had. Jimmy gave his dad and I a lift home, as it was too icy for us to walk back, for which we were very grateful.

Reminiscing afterwards I wonder what it is that makes some functions so successful and happy. The atmosphere at the party was uplifting. Between Christmas and New Year had all Christine's life to be a bad time to have a birthday but that party made it the very best time to have a party. Margaret went home the next day.

New Year's Eve 2000 and Jim and I have resigned our selves to having a quiet New Year's Eve. Times and customs are changing. Gone are the days of open house on the last night of the year. You never know who is around these days.

The Residents Association is thriving. Christine is now chairperson having been secretary for two years. East and North have had streets pulled down. Both have had bungalows built among the houses. We are asked why we do not want to move to a bungalow. The most persuasive argument against is the open view to the front of our house.

The coastal view day and night is constantly changing. The moon shining on the sea on a dark night reflecting its mysterious light to and creating a silver path to the land is a wonder to look at. Some days to watch the sunbeams twinkling like diamonds on the sea is worth more than gold. On stormy days I can imagine serpents and weird, prehistoric creatures thrashing about under the sea causing turmoil in the form of roaring waves and stirring, frothy foam. Perhaps it is an old seagod throwing a rock from the bottom of the wild sea into the air and watching with glee splash back into the water causing a mile high column of wild white bubbles to fly into the sky. Another thing we own this house and would pay rent in a bungalow, as they are not for sale. Also we have so many things we would not get them into a small place. We love this house the rooms are large and airy. Half a street opposite us has been demolished. Some streets have been refurbished and are still empty. The state of some streets in South is such I wish there was some way of getting to Seaside Lane without passing them with their boarded up houses, yard walls down, rubbish strewn about and the air of despair and dereliction that goes with it. I am in a trap.

We decided to have a new brick yard. I phoned Rick to check if any work was going to be carried out in this street in the future in case the next European funding would include improvements to Boston street which would make it worthwhile hanging on for awhile before embarking on the expense of a new yard. Rick said, go ahead as in the future money was going to be used for demolition. Good this is the best thing for us in the South block of houses. Many people who live in the derelict streets have expressed the desire to have the streets demolished as this will make them have to move and any move for them must be for the better they tell me.

We have our new yard. It is very smart. Jim now has the interest of planning plants for the yard where we sit on fine summer days. I love those days when I sit in the warmth of the sun, reading, writing, painting or just dreaming. Toby is a joy and a pleasure to have.

Alex has been to see us telling us of Princess Helena's divorce and how he had feelings for her and they are now married. It is like a fairytale, he brought Princess Helena on another visit and promised not to loose touch in the future.

I am asked sometimes how I see the future of Easington. Well how I would like to see it is as a small coastal village with our seashore and cliffs an attraction with wild life and rare plants. The pit site to be a walkway with trees, sculptures, some of fossilised trees and leaves such as seen down the pit, a history of the place to be inserted on plaques with the names of all who were killed at the pit. Also a memorial to those injured and those who died through industrial diseases. A building on the site with local crafts and books for sale. In this building a little café with home made snacks on the menu. A house or two converted into a museum.

On Halloween night a ghostly walk across the fields (for the very fit) carrying lanterns, meeting up with the rest at the farm and there holding a folk night with songs poetry all about ghostly happenings with snacks of Pumpkin pie, Witches Brew, and Frog Spawn (tapioca) and Bat Pie and so on. Everyone in fancy dress as witches, skeletons, etc.

Also houses advertised in other parts of the country as holiday cottages and enough entertainment to entice them. People have holiday homes in the Lakes, why not here. We could have trips to sea travelling down the coast to Whitby, fishing trips. I could think of many more. There was an article about me in the Mail about ten years ago in which I forecast the closure of the pit as I had written a poem to the effect of how I would see us in the future as a holiday place.

We need a first class place to eat and stay.

This brings me up to date – the beginning of March and the weather is bitterly cold.

CHAPTER THIRTY SIX

OCTOBER 19th 2002

I am 72 years old. So many things have happened in Easington since the pit closed. Easington Colliery no longer feels like home. People are moving away. We lock our doors at all times and are suspicious of strangers. Shoplifting is a common occurrence in the local shops. Drug raids on houses occur.

We have had flowers stolen from the back yard so many times we no longer bother to try to make the place look pretty.

Streets in North and South i.e. the A and B streets are being demolished. Some have already gone in the C streets of East. We understand our house is due for demolition sometime which gives me a strange feeling to think our lovely welcoming home will be no more.

Jim and I will move to a bungalow. Away from Easington. This would have upset me a few years ago but now I feel emotionless about it.

Christine is receptionist at the resource centre in Easington Colliery. Margaret has moved from Devon to Sedgefield and is a Schools Inspector for County Durham. Jim Jnr. Is a Senior Engineer at Nissan. Stuart moved from Carlisle to Meadowfield and is Senior Technical Officer in Cardiology at Durham University Hospital. Dawn is I.T. support worker at E.D.S. which is a call centre. Dominic is following in his fathers footsteps and is training at Nissan. Becky is at Durham College studying Hairdressing and Beauty Treatment and works in a Hairdressing Salon at weekends and holidays.

I continue to keep writing and learning. My family continues to see that I keep abreast of the times. My latest gadget is a mobile phone which Margaret brought for me.

I am going to buy a digital camera so that Jim can take photos which is a hobby of his and I then can print them through the computer. I have to learn how to do this.

I have bought a dictation machine, a new name for a tape recorder as I intend for my next project to collect life stories of other people in Easington and the surrounding pit areas and have them published so there will be an account of ordinary every day life of how lived, played, worked and loved in our pit villages.

The way I see the future of Easington Colliery is to demolish all old houses and buildings and leave green fields for a while and then think for a long time very carefully what to do with the land.

Look for my star in the sky at the head of Pegasus and remember me.

EASINGTON PIT
FEB. 17TH 1900- MAY 1993
Men and Boys killed

No.	Name	Age	Occupation	Date killed	Details (if any)
1	Robert Arthur	22	Sinker	17.2.1900	A full kibble of stones was taken up too high, the detaching hook acted alright, but one of the links below it broke and the kibble fell into the shaft and killed him.
2	William James Curry	25	Sinker	17.2.1900	Same as above. A kibble is 4 feet in diameter by 4 feet deep and weighed when full about 4 and a half tons. A link in the chain broke.
3	Thomas Milburn Jameson	26	Cartman	21.10.1901	He was driving a horse which was pulling a tip waggon(sic) from tip end towards shaft when by some means he fell in from off the waggon (sic) and was ran over and killed
4	Robert Atkinson	56	Sinker	1904	While sinking the shaft was buried in quicksand 28th Nov.1904 body recovered 18th Feb 1909.

No.	Name	Age	Occupation	Date killed	Details (if any)
5	Stephen Griffen	32	Sinker	19.5.1911	The Deceased and 11 others under the supervision of the master sinker ere placing in position a balk 30ft. long by 12inches the derrick was on a ledge holding the balk, it slipped and Griffen was carried down and crushed under the balk.
6	Martin Hart	33	Labourer	30.6.1911	He was engaged with his brother on a scaffold 23feet from the ground scraping and cleaning the iron girders of a new heapstead and making them ready for concrete; the scaffold consisted of one or more planks resting on projecting poles and they were moved about as required; the accident was due to the deceased attempting to move a plank without assistance when it fell off the pole at the other end and he overbalanced himself and fell on to some loose girders which were lying on the ground

No.	Name	Age	Occupation	Date killed	Details (if any)
7	Thomas Moseby	22	Hewer	24.7.1912	He was in the act of setting a prop, and was driving it up when it bounced back and released a large quantity of stone from the roof, it was afterwards seen that the roof contained a mass of fossils, a most unusual occurrence in this seam; this accident had the effect of reducing the maximum timbering distance in that seam.
8	John W. Nichol	23	Screener: (coal cleaner) sic	18.8.1913	(Accident 7.8.1913)deceased told the heap keeper that his knee had been crushed between the tubs and showed him the bruises: no one saw the accident: his duty was to regulate the empty tubs gravitating to the shaft and he had to move the suitable levers, and may quite easily have been nipped as he described. He died 18.8.1913.
9	Jack Lambton			20.11.1913	Fell off South pit engine house
10	George Robinson	44	Hewer	3.4.1914	Deceased was driving a leading heading through two rise faults, when a sudden outburst of coal and gas occurred. He was partly buried and before he was rescued he became asphyxiated. (sic)
11	George Lambton		Traffic Manager	4.12.1914	Killed by Loco

No.	Name	Age	Occupation	Date killed	Details (if any)
12	Richard Young	45	Deputy	21.4.1914	Deceased and another deputy were assisting to clear a fall when a small piece of stone fell which struck him.
13	William Hardy	45	Hewer	14.12.1914	Killed by fall of stone
14	Owen Owens	30	Hewer	14.2.1916	Killed by fall of stone
15	John Neasham 5, 2nd Street, East	48		23.3.1916	
16	Robert Ridley	19	Putter	17.9.1916	
17	Abraham Wayman	22	Hewer	2.10.1916	
18	Robert Herring	42	Stone Tippler	5.3.1917	
19	Edward Bowman	42	Stoneman	24.6.1917	
20	Richard Merritt 4, 6th Street North	44	Chock drawer	0.7.1917	Killed by a fall of stone.
21	Patrick Gilmore 24, Station Road	22	Hewer	13.9.1917	Injuries lifting a tub. Coroner's jury verdict – cause of death was injury to back and kidneys caused while lifting a tub
22	Thomas Morris	15	Driver	26.10.1917	Accident 22.10.1917. Crushed between a tub and a prop
23	J.W.(N) Raper	18	Engine lad	25.11.1917	Killed at 3rd West Low Main Seam by a fall of stone (spine fractured)
24	Thomas Mothersill 85, Station Road	20		1917	Killed at 2nd North Main Coal Seam
25	William Bell 6, 5th Street North	52	Hewer	4.7.1918	Killed by fall of stone at East Flat Hutton Seam
26	Jos. Vickers 13, 13th Street North	15		23.9.1918	
27	Robert Todd	55	Hewer	31.10.1919	Struck on head by piece of stone
28	J.C. Robson	19	Labourer on screens	13.3.1920	Through a fall of stone
29	John Pearce	56	Hewer	14.3.1920	Caught by a set while dressing

No.	Name	Age	Occupation	Date killed	Details (if any)
30	Allan Hocking	19		4.5.1920	Killed at Low Main Incline Hutton Seam
31	John G. Carter	22	Putter	14.7.1920	Fall of stone
32	Stephen Kirk	67	Stoneman	18.9.1920	Fall of stone
33	Joseph Sennet	23	Stoneman	31.8.1921	Fall of stone
34	John Tulip	48	Hewer	8.12.1921	Fall of stone
35	John Robert Robson	16	Landing lad	2.7.1922	Crushed by set
36	John Tulip	20	Putter	17.12.1923	Was found lying unconscious i.e. dead on travelling way
37	J.Ellwood		Deputy	27.10.1925	Run over
38	M. Leadbitter	52	Timber drawer	10.3.1926	Roof fall
39	T. Meakin	14½	Landing boy	21.3.1927	Caught by set.
40	J. Daglish		Hewer	17.5.1927	Roof fall
41	T.B. Grieves	27	Cutter	18.5.1927	Fall of stone
42	J.W. Henderson	28	Hewer	31.8.1928	Fall of coal
43	S. Jackson	14½	Shaft hand	21.2.1929	Caught by tubs
44	H. Bell	16	Landing boy	22.2.1929	He was lowering set of full tubs controlled by drags, from the main haulage towards the shaft. As the moving set approached the standing tubs he attempted to couple them and his head was crushed between the tubs.
45	J. Elland		Hewer	7.3.1929	Roof fall
46	G.G. Turner	15½	Engine boy	4.10.1929	Caught by engine
47	H. Wilson	36	Hewer	7.10.1929	Caught by set
48	Arthur Chambers	20	Haulage boy	13.10.1930	Caught by tubs
49	Thomas Simpson	24	Putter	29.2.1932	Found dead under tub of coal
50	Joseph James	33	Coal hewer	13.8.1932	Fall of stone
51	Albert Aitkenhead Lived at Horden	30	Stoneman	14.10.1932	Fall of roof
52	John Littler	25	Coal hewer	16.11.1932	Fall of stone

No.	Name	Age	Occupation	Date killed	Details (if any)
53	George Robert Barker	45	Coal hewer	13.4.1933	Fall of stone
54	Miles Handy	56	Stoneman	24.4.1933	Hit by fallen prop
55	James Thomas Gray	58	Deputy	10.11.1933	
56	William Robson	15	Datal lad	11.12.1933	Caught by set of tubs
57	Joseph Honour	45	Machine man	7.5.1934	Found under coal cutting machine. Fall of stone.
58	Stanley Harris	25	Putter	15.12.1934	Fell in pit
59	Elisha Potter	57	Canchman	13.11.1934	Fall of stone in return
60	S. Harris	25	Putter	15.12.1934	
61	M. Reilly	56	Stoneman	6.3.1935	Died from injuries
62	Thomas Clough	37		20'4.1935	Died from injuries received
63	J.H.Morton	27	Driller	15.1.1936	Fall of stone. He as wearing a safety helmet at the time but a stone went straight through it
64	William Dunn	53		13.2.1936	
65	Anthony Gray	36	Filler	17.3.1936	Fall of rumble
66	Ernest Watson	38	Conveyor man	5.10.1936	Found gassed in the in bye side of a fenced off place
67	A.B.Cairns	34	Timber drawer	23.12.1936	Caught by fall of stone
68	R. Mawhinney	45	Hewer	1.8.1937	Accident 2.10.1931, killed by a fall of stone
69	R.N.Whinning	45	Hewer	1.8.1937	
70	James B. A. Raper	63	Wasteman	24.9.1937	Presumed hit by tubs
71	K. Goodwin	34	Hewer	21.10.1937	Fall of stone
72	Lancelot Turnbull	44	Hewer	22.11.1937	Fall of stone
73	Geo. B. Whiting	32	Stoneman	22.11.1937	Fall of stone
74	John Golightly	47	Hewer	2.2.1938	Fall of stone
75	James A. Daglish Westmoreland	34	Stoneman	16.12.1938	Struck with a prop that was knocked out by a piece of stone in return airway
76	Wm. Robinson	56	Shaftman	2.2.1940	Working in shaft on cage when it made a move and he lost his balance and fell off cage down shaft

A Chronicle of Easington Colliery

No.	Name	Age	Occupation	Date killed	Details (if any)
77	Thomas Wheatley Collingwood	27		14.10.1940	Crushed by tubs at separation doors while operating clip
78	Daniel Ward	48	Timber yard worker	3.7.1941	Fractured finger while carrying a 7 foot prop died as a result of Tetanus 16.7.1941
79	James Williams	40	Surface labourer	23.1.1942	Crushed under lift at bank
80	Clifford Scott	41	Drawer	20.10.1942	Fall of post stone while drawing a bord (sic)
81	Evan Ames	50	Coal hewer	23.10.1942	Fall of roof at the face of lift
82	G.W. Elliott	50		29.7.1944	Fall of stone
83	John Holden	43	Shifter	29.9.1944	Fall of roof
84	John Bee	72	Surface labourer	26.3.1946	Fell from gantry while tightening up hydraulic ram glands
85	George Goodrum	31	Hewer	26.4.1946	Found under first tub of four while putting
86	J.H.Robinson	42		12.6.1946	Run over by men riding set of tubs
87	W. Powers	38	Stoneman	25.9.1946	Lifting tub
88	T..Williams	70	Shifter	25.3.1947	accident 3.3.1947 and heart failure
89	Arthur Jones Lived at Wheatley Hill	34	Shifter	16.12.1947	Crushed between tub and timber tram
90	Joseph Deighton	25	Pony putter	8.1.1948	Injured by tubs in landing
91	J. Cruddace	49	Hewer	2.2.1948	Accident 2.2.1948. and pneumoconiosis
92	T. Bewick		Hewer	1.11.1950	Accident 1.11.1943 and pneumoconiosis

DISASTER MAY 29TH 1951

An explosion occurred in the FIVE QUARTER SEAM known as THE DUCKBILLS at 4.35am. when there were two shifts of men in the district. 38 belonging to 10 o'clock shift (stoneman shift) and 43 to 3.40am. (foreshift).

THESE ARE THE NAMES OF THE MEN KILLED.

No.	Name	Age	Occupation	Date killed	Details (if any)
93	John Anson	64	Shifter		
94	William Armstrong	55	Datal		
95	Mark Smart Bedding	38	Filler		
96	Matthew Blevins	27	Filler		
97	George Brenkley	20	Filler		
98	Thomas Brenkley	32	Filler		
99	Louis Brennan	49	Stoneman		
100	George Miller Brown	50	Datal		
101	Bertram Burn	25	Filler		
102	Emmerson Cain	63	Stoneman		
103	Frederick Cairns	23	Filler		
104	George Calvert	50	Stoneman		
105	James Calvin	51	Conveyor maintenance		
106	Frederick Carr	50	Electrician		
107	George William Carr	45	Timber drawer		
108	James Carr	38	Timber drawer		
109	John Edwin Challoner	53	Deputy		
110	Richard Champley	43	Cutter		
111	Albert Kerr Chapman	44	Stoneman		
112	Joseph Charlton	42	Master Shifter		
113	John Clough	57	Shifter		
114	William Arthur Dryden	27	Filler		
115	John Ellison	19	Datal		
116	Charles Fishburn	54	Shifter		
117	Henry Fishburn	23	Filler		
118	Thomas Garside	20	Datal		
119	Joseph Godsman	41	Cutter		

No.	Name	Age	Occupation	Date killed	Details (if any)
120	George Goulburn	57	Mason's labourer		
121	Albert Gowland	51	Deputy		
122	Ernest Goyns	60	Stoneman		
123	Herbert Goyns	56	Stoneman		
124	John Harker	53	Shifter		
125	John William Henderson	56	Shifter		
126	Thomas Heppell	31	Filler		
127	Daniel Hunt	54	Datal		
128	Stephen Hunt	24	Filler		
129	William Hunt	43	Datal		
130	Arthur Chambers Hutton	42	Filler		
131	Frederick Ernest Jepson	68	Shifter		
132	Lawrence Jones	36	Filler		
133	Thomas Edward Jones	35	Deputy		
134	Herbert Jeffrey Jobling	57	Shifter		
135	John Kelly	57	Datal		
136	William Kelly	28	Filler		
137	John Edward Armstrong Lamb	43	Datal		
138	Jesse Stephenson Link	44	Datal		
139	Joseph Fairless Lippeatt	37	Filler		
140	Peter Lynch	20	Filler		
141	Denis McRoy	23	Filler		
142	William James McRoy	31	Filler		
143	Robert William Milburn	26	Filler		
144	Harold Nelson	49	Stoneman		
145	Albert Newcombe	67	Stoneman		
146	Norman Nicholson	29	Filler		
147	Robert Noble	45	Shifter		
148	William Parkin	24	Filler		
149	William Edward Forbes Parks	62	Shifter		
150	Robert Pase	63	Shifter		
151	Stanley Peaceful	37	Stoneman		
152	Alexander Penman	42	Cutter		

No.	Name	Age	Occupation	Date killed	Details (if any)
153	James Porter	32	Filler		
154	John Thomas Porter	23	Filler		
155	Thomas Valentine Rice	53	Shifter		
156	John Robinson	50	Shifter		
157	John George Robson	25	Filler		
158	George Scott	53	Datal		
159	Albert Seymour	64	Datal		
160	Frederick Sillito	52	Shifter		
161	George Henry Stubbs	60	Shifter		
162	Hugh Bell Surtees	36	Datal		
163	Matthew White Surtees	61	Shifter		
164	Lawrence Thompson	54	Datal		
165	Thomas Thompson	28	Underground Bricklayer		
166	Thomas Trisnan	43	Stoneman		
167	Robert Turnbull	64	Master Wasteman		
168	George Wilkie	63	Shifter		
169	Reginald Wilkinson	40	Stoneman		
170	Robert Willins	45	Foreoverman		
171	Matthew Williams	18	Datal		Fatally injured died same day
172	John Wilson	62	Hauling engineman		
173	Stephen Wilson	60	Shifter		
174	John Young Wallace	26	Back overman Rescue worker		Overcome by noxious gas same day
175	Henry Burdess	43	Deputy Rescue worker		Overcome by noxious gas 1st June 1951

MEN KILLED SINCE 1951

No.	Name	Age	Occupation	Date killed	Details (if any)
176	Norman Eales	47	Surface Hand	6.4.1953	Injured by blow on head while climbing ladder out of stone bunker – died
177	Arthur Elliott	15	Surface Hand	19.5.1953	Head caught by lift gate which is raised by lift cage
178	Thomas S. Carr	27	Puller	16.7.1954	Fall of stone while drawing
179	Herbert S. Hall	47	Coal Cutter	14.9.1955	Fall of stone
180	J. Handy	23	Coal Filler	4.1.1956	Struck by overlapping coal knocked on to chain conveyor
181	George F. Harriman	43	Puller	18.10.1957	Fractured jaw, ribs and legs
182	Charles Dedman	42	Tippler Operator	26.12.1961	Found with head crushed between tippler and 3 ton mine car
183	T. McGoldrick	56	Diesel Tractor Driver	19.6.1965	Head trapped by tube and tractor. Ventilation tube was too low
184	George Hancock		Power Loader	22.5.1967	Trapped by girder caught by a fall of stone when drawing girder
185	J.A.Musgrove	23	Power Loader	20.1.1968	Head trapped between girder and top of machine in stenton
186	Billy Challoner	47		18.7.1969	Removing stage loader when roof began to work. A major fall in advanced heading at the stenton junction. Fall 26ft 9 inches E.W. 23ft N.S.10ft high
187	Robert Fenwick	48		18.7.1969	Same as above

No.	Name	Age	Occupation	Date killed	Details (if any)
188	Stephen Knapper	16	Surface Hand	15.6.1971	Trapped in machinery at coal processing plant
189	W. Morris	61	Banksman	18.4.1975	
190	W. Hogg	19	Underground	15.8.1980	Killed while transporting materials to the face in the High Main
191	R. Frecker	21	Underground	1.12.1980	Killed by airlock doors
192	Jonathan Wylie	32	Power Loader	14.3.1991	Roof Collapse

Researched with great difficulty by Mary N. Bell. I sincerely hope I have been able to find every man killed at Easington Colliery. Apologies if I missed anyone.

Printed in Great Britain
by Amazon.co.uk, Ltd.,
Marston Gate.